Strategies for Learning

If we are serious about Arabic reading mastery we must begin by rejecting the myth that Arabic is hard. By doing this we will begin to remove subconscious obstacles in our learning process. Like any language Arabic takes Practice.

This book was designed to be both Classroom Ready and compatible with Home Study.

Common Techniques:

▶ Read and ask students to follow along silently
▶ Select individual students to read the text aloud
▶ Ask the class to read the text aloud together
▶ Write text on the board and call on students to read it
▶ Read and ask students to repeat

CONTENTS

Section 1 : Sounds of the Letters

In This Section

▶ Introduction to the sounds of the letters
▶ Practice Exercises
▶ Knowledge Self Test

 We will begin by mastering the letter sounds.

THE ARABIC ALPHABET

SOUND	LETTER	NAME	SOUND	LETTER	NAME
r	ر	raa	a	ا	alif
z	ز	zaay	b	ب	baa
s	س	seen	t	ت	taa
sh	ش	sheen	th	ث	thaa
ṣ	ص	ṣawd	j	ج	jeem
ḍ	ض	ḍawd	H	ح	Haa
ṭ	ط	ṭaa	kh	خ	Khaa
ẓ	ظ	ẓaa	d	د	daal
'a	ع	'ayn	dh	ذ	dhaal

4

SOUND	LETTER	NAME	SOUND	LETTER	NAME
m	م	meem	g	غ	ghayn
n	ن	noon	f	ف	faa
h * also written as	ه هـ	haa	q	ق	qaaf
w	و	waaw	k	كـ	kaaf
y	ي	yaa	l	ل	laam

2

Pronunciation Chart

a	ا	a as in **a**pple
b	ب	b as in **b**at
t	ت	t as in **t**ap
th	ث	tha as in **th**ing
j	ج	j as in **j**am
H	ح	H is a heavy H
kh	خ	kh exhaled from the throat
d	د	d as in **d**ad
dh	ذ	dh as in **th**ere
r	ر	r as in **r**aw
z	ز	z as in **z**ebra
s	س	s as in **s**ing
sh	ش	sh as in **sh**ape

3

sw	ص	saw as in **saw**
dw	ض	daw as in **daw**n
tw	ط	taw as in **tau**ght
zw	ظ	zaw as in **zaw**
ʻe	ع	e as in **eye**
g	غ	g as in **guy**
f	ف	f as in **f**amily
q	ق	q as in **q**uarter
k	ك	k as in **k**ite
l	ل	l as in **l**augh
m	م	m as in **m**ake
n	ن	n as in **n**oon
h	ه	h as in **ha**ppy
w	و	w as in **wo**w
y	ي	y as in **y**ou

4

Arabic is read from Right to Left

Right to Left

It is crucial to become comfortable with the right to left orientation of Arabic script. Arabic is written from right to left. Read each line from the right. When you finish reading each line begin the next at the right again.

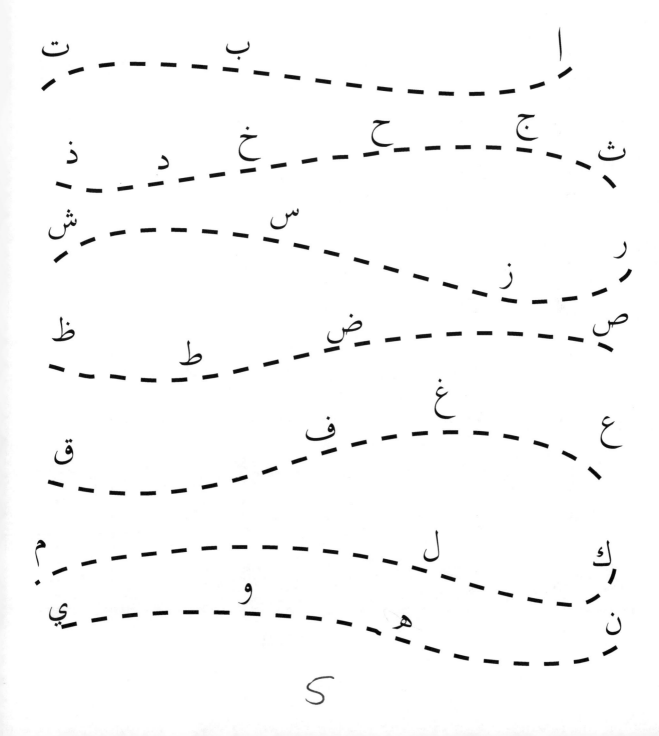

5

Letter Recognition Exercise 1.1
Read each row from right to left.

ا غ ا ت د ع ذ ض س ر ذ د ز ز س
a a g t d r dh dw s r dh d z z s

ا ف ا ف ا ز ج د ح خ ت ب ا ب ث
th b a t kh h d j z a f a f a th

ب ف ذ ض ص ش ص س ر ب ا غ
g a b r s sh sw dw dh f b

ب ا ر د ج خ ح ط ا ظ ا ظ ا ظ ظ
zw a zw a zw a zw a th j kh h d r a b

ز و ظ ص ث ش ش م ت ن ه و ز
z w n th sh sw zw n z

ب ر ش و ظ ض ذ س ه ت ن م
m n t h dh dw zw w sh r b

ز ك ر ز ل ض ك ذ ص ش س
s s sh sw dh k dw l z r k z

ب ا ع ض ص ع ق ا ق ا ق ا ق ا
a g a q a q a q sw dw a q b

Letter Recognition Exercise 1.2

Read each row from right to left.

esvohgod

 س ا ز ا ز ا ز ا ز ا ز ا ز ا ز ا ز ح ت ا خ
kh a t h z a z a z a z a z a z a s

ح ج ا خ ا خ ت د د ج د ح ت خ د ج ا خ
kh akh akh t d j dh t kh d j h

خ د ت د ب ا ت د خ د ت د ج ح د خ
kh d b a t d kh d t d j h d kh

ت د ا ب ث ا خ ا ج ا ب ث د د
t d a b th b a kh a j a b th d d

ر د ا ر ح خ د ج ح ا ذ ا ذ ا ذ ا ذ
r d r a r h kh d j h a dh a dh a dh a dh

ا ا ج ا ب ث ذ ج ح خ ا ذ ذ ذ ذ ت
a a j a b th dh j h kh a dh dh d dh t

ح ج د ر د ب ث ذ ب ا ر ا ر ا ر ا ر
b th dh b th a r a r a r a r d j h

خ ح د ذ ث س س ا س س ا س ا ز ا
a z a s s a s th dh dh h kh

Letter Recognition Exercise 1.3

Read each row from right to left.

- -

س ا ذ س ذ ز س ز س ج س خ س

ش ا ش ا ش ا ش ا ث س س ا ش ا ر س ا

ص ا ح ت د س ذ ش خ ذ ر ش

ص ر ش س س ذ س ر ذ ز ر ح ج خ ا ص ا

س ص ر ا ص ا ذ ث ص ص ش

ض ا ض ا ض ا ض ا ض ص س س ذ ش

ب ت ز ر ض د ض د ض د د ذ س

ب ا خ ت ز ر ب ا ذ ض ذ ض ا ا

Letter Recognition Exercise 1.4

Read each row from right to left.

· ·

ط ا ط ا ط ا ط ض ص ا ض ذ ث

tw a tw a tw a sw dw a dw dh th

د ط ذ ض ا خ ح ط ن ا ت ط س ا

a s tw t n a tw dh t j kh a tw s a

ا ا ظ ا ذ ث ب ا ت ز ز ز ط ت ج

j t tw z z z th/dh a ʒ t a zw a a

ظ ا ر ب ا ظ ا ظ ا ط ج خ ح د ر ا ب ظ

a zw a zw a zw a tw j kh h d r a b zw

ع ب ا ت ز ر ذ ع ج د ح ر ز ر ش

sh r z h d j ʒe dh r z t a b ʒe

ت ث ب ر ذ ع ا ج ع ا ح ع خ

kh ʒe h ʒe j a ʒe dh r b th t

ا غ ا ت د ع ذ ض ر س ر ذ ز س

s z dh r s dw dh ʒe d t a g a

س ص ع س ر ز ع ح ا غ ا غ غ

g g ʒe sw r z ʒe h a g a g g

Letter Recognition Exercise 1.5

Read each row from right to left.

غ ا غ ع ذ س ش ق ص ظ ز ق

س ش ض ث ب ق ا ت خ ح د ج

خ غ ق ت ع ق غ ق ب ل ر ز ق

ل ع ا ي ا ي ا ي ا ي ز و ى

ف ا غ ع ق ف ذ ا ظ غ ق ح غ ق

ا ك ا ك ا ك ا ك ا ب ا غ ش س ث

ر ب ف ك ذ ض ص ش س ر ك

ك د ع ف ا ر ذ ح ج د خ ت ز ك

Letter Recognition Exercise 1.6
Read each row from right to left.

ب ك ل ا ل ا ل ا ل ا ل ا ل ا ذ ل ظ ط

ز ك ر ز ل ض ك ذ ك ض ل ز ر ك ز ش ش س س

غ ع ل ق ف ث ل س ب ل س ا ل ت ر

ا س ل ب ل ك ل ز ظ ط ج د ح خ

ل ب ا و ت ج د ط ك ظ ز ك ظ

ز و ظ ص ث ش ش م ت ن ه و ز

ب ر ش و ظ ض ذ س ه ت ن م

ل ى و ز ا ي ا ي ا ي ا ي ا ي ا ع و ل

Letter Recognition Exercise 1.7
Read each row from right to left.

د ظ ط ج ك م ب خ ه ع ا ث ا ر

ي م ا ل خ ر ذ ي س ا ز ض ج

ب ي ا ت ع ه ي و غ ض ز ظ

ا ا ت ب ت ا ث ن م ب س ه ش

ظ و ز ي ر ذ ض ص ث ت ث ت ا

ح ط ا ن ت ط ب ف ك ذ ض م ك

خ ت ز ك ر ت ج د ط ذ ض ا خ

ط ا ي ذ ف ض ص ث ك ح د ج

Letter Review Exercise A

Complete the Alphabet Chart. Fill in the boxes with the missing letters.

خ			ث		ب	ا
		س		ر		
	ف		ع		ط	
ي		ه				ك

 Did you know that at one time the Arabic Alphabet was written in a different order?

Letter Review Exercise B

Complete the Alphabet Chart. Fill in the boxes with the missing letters.

		ج				
	ش		ز		ذ	
					ط	
					ل	

 Did you know that the word Alphabet originates from the names of the first three letters of the Arabic Alphabet 'alif' 'ba' 'ta'?

Name the letter.

	ق		Ba	ب
	ن			و
	م			غ
	ث			ك
	ر			ذ
	ه			ي
	س			ظ
	ض			ح
	ت			ل

Section 2: The Short Vowels

In This Section
- ▶ Introduction to the short vowels
- ▶ Combining the letters with vowel sounds
- ▶ Reading Practice
- ▶ Fluency Activity
- ▶ Knowledge Self Test

 We will now take our first step in reading by working with the letters in combination with vowels.

Fat-ha

Fatha is a short vowel that is written as a slanted line above the letter. Fat-ha makes a short [a] sound like the 'a' in apple.

$$a = \underline{}\ \acute{}\ \text{ Fat-ha}$$

What happens when we combine the sound of the letters with the short vowel Fat-ha?

بَ = بْ = ب

Ba   **a**   **B**

Da	ضَ	Ka	كَ
Ta	طَ	Ya	يَ
Ra	رَ	Ha	حَ
Za	زَ	Tha	ثَ
Sa	سَ	Ja	جَ
Fa	فَ	La	لَ
Ma	مَ	Kha	خَ

Kasra

Kasra is a short vowel that is written as a slanted line below the letter. Kasra makes a short [i] sound like the 'i' in 'sit'.

$$i = \underline{\hspace{2cm}}\; Kasra$$

What happens when we combine the sound of the letters with the short vowel Kasra ?

بِ = ِ ب

Bi   **i**   **B**

Ji	جِ	Ri	رِ
Mi	مِ	Thi	ثِ
Zi	ظِ	hi	هِ
Khi	خِ	Bi	بِ
Wi	وِ	Ki	كِ
Ti	تِ	Di	دِ
Hi	حِ	Ni	نِ

Damma

Damma is a short vowel that is written as a loop above the letter. Damma makes a short [u] sound like the 'u' in bus.

$$u = \underline{\quad ُ \quad} \text{ Damma}$$

What happens when we combine the sound of the letters with the short vowel Damma?

$$بُ = ُ \quad ب$$

Bu   **u**   **B**

Nu	نُ	Zu	زُ
Mu	مُ	Du	ضُ
Su	سُ	Gu	غُ
Ju	جُ	Yu	يُ
Khu	خُ	hu	هُ
Lu	لُ	Tu	تُ
Fu	فُ	Bu	بُ

Read each row from right to left.

أُ	ا	أَ	ا	أَ	أُ
	إِ		إِ	إِ	

أُ	أَ	ا	أُ	أَ	ا
		إِ			إِ

أَ	ا	ا	أَ	ا	أَ
	إِ	إِ		إِ	

ا	أَ	أَ	ا	أُ	أَ
إِ			إِ		

أُ	أَ	أَ	أُ	ا	أُ
				إِ	

ا	ا	أَ	أُ	أَ	ا
إِ	إِ	ا	ا	ا	إِ

أُ	أُ	ا	أُ	أَ
ا	ا	إِ	ا	ا

Read each row from right to left.

بُ بَ بِ بَ بِ بُ

بِ بُ بِ بِ بُ بُ

بَ بَ بُ بِ بَ بِ

بُ بُ بَ بُ بَ بَ

بِ بَ بِ بَ بِ بِ

بِ بِ بُ بِ بَ بِ

بَ بُ بَ بَ بُ بَ

بَ بُ بَ بَ بُ بُ

Read each row from right to left.

تَ تُ تِ تُ تَ تِ

تَ تَ تِ تُ تَ تُ

تِ تَ تِ تُ تِ تَ

تُ تِ تَ تُ تَ تُ

تِ تِ تُ تَ تِ تَ

تَ تُ تَ تِ تِ تِ

تُ تِ تُ تَ تِ تُ

تَ تُ تَ تِ تِ تُ

Read each row from right to left.

ثُ ثِ ثُ ثَ ثَ ثِ

ثِ ثَ ثُ ثُ ثِ ثُ

ثِ ثَ ثُ ثِ ثِ ثُ

ثَ ثِ ثُ ثِ ثِ ثُ

ثُ ثِ ثَ ثُ ثِ ثِ

ثِ ثُ ثُ ثِ ثِ ثَ

ثِ ثِ ثُ ثَ ثُ ثَ

ثِ ثُ ثَ ثُ ثِ ثَ

Read each row from right to left.

خَ   خِ   خَ   خِ   خُ   خَ

حُ   حِ   حِ   حُ   حَ   حِ

خِ   خَ   خُ   خَ   خَ   خُ

حَ   حُ   حَ   خَ   خُ   خِ

حُ   خَ   حَ   خَ   حَ   خُ

حُ   حَ   حُ   حِ   حَ   خُ

حِ   حِ   حِ   خَ   خُ   خَ

Read each row from right to left.

خَ	خُ	حَ	خِ	حِ	خَ
حِ	خَ	خِ	حِ	خَ	حِ
خَ	خُ	خُ	خَ	حَ	خُ
حِ	خُ	حَ	خُ	حَ	خَ
خَ	خَ	خُ	حَ	خُ	حَ
حَ	خَ	خَ	خُ	حَ	خَ
خَ	خَ	حَ	خَ	خَ	خُ

Read each row from right to left.

خُ   خَ   خُ   خُ   خِ   خَ

خَ   خَ   خَ   خُ   خَ   خَ

خَ   خَ   خَ   خَ   خُ   خُ

خُ   خُ   خُ   خَ   خَ   خَ

خَ   خَ   خَ   خُ   خَ   خَ

خَ   خَ   خَ   خَ   خُ   خَ

خُ   خُ   خَ   خَ   خَ   خُ

Short vowels [a] [i] [u]   **Practice Exercise 2.8**

Read each row from right to left.

دِ	دَ	دَ	دُ	دَ
دِ	دُ	دِ	دَ	دِ
دَ	دَ	دَ	دُ	دُ
دَ	دَ	دُ	دَ	دِ
دُ	دَ	دُ	دَ	دِ
دَ	دُ	دَ	دَ	دِ
دَ	دَ	دُ	دَ	دِ
دُ	دَ	دُ	دُ	دَ

Read each row from right to left.

نَ نِ　　　نَ نِ　　　نَ نِ　　　نُ نِ　　　نَ نِ

نُ نَ　　　نَ نِ　　　نُ نِ　　　نَ نِ　　　نُ نِ

نَ نِ　　　نَ نِ　　　نَ نِ　　　نُ نِ　　　نَ نِ

نِ نَ　　　نُ نِ　　　نِ نَ　　　نُ نِ　　　نِ نَ

نِ نَ　　　نِ نَ　　　نُ نَ　　　نِ نَ　　　نُ نِ

نُ نَ　　　نُ نَ　　　نِ نَ　　　نَ نِ　　　نِ نَ

نُ نِ　　　نَ نِ　　　نَ نِ　　　نُ نَ　　　نَ نِ

Read each row from right to left.

رَ	رُ	رَ	رِ	رِ
رِ	رَ	رِ	رَ	رُ
رَ	رِ	رُ	رِ	رَ
رُ	رَ	رَ	رِ	رُ
رِ	رَ	رُ	رَ	رِ
رَ	رِ	رِ	رُ	رَ
رِ	رِ	رَ	رِ	رُ
رُ	رَ	رُ	رَ	رَ

Read each row from right to left.

زُ	زَ	زِ	زَ	زُ	زَ	زِ
زِ	زُ	زَ	زِ	زُ	زُ	زُ
زُ	زِ	زِ	زُ	زَ	زِ	زَ
زِ	زُ	زُ	زُ	زَ	زَ	زِ
زُ	زِ	زِ	زَ	زُ	زَ	زُ
زُ	زَ	زُ	زَ	زِ	زُ	زِ
زَ	زُ	زِ	زَ	زَ	زِ	زَ

Read each row from right to left.

سَ	سِ	سَ	سُ	سُ	سِ
سِ	سَ	سِ	سَ	سَ	سُ
سِ	سَ	سِ	سُ	سِ	سَ
سِ	سَ	سُ	سِ	سَ	سُ
سَ	سَ	سِ	سَ	سُ	سِ
سُ	سِ	سَ	سِ	سِ	سُ
سَ	سُ	سِ	سَ	سُ	سَ

Read each row from right to left.

شَ	شَ	شُ	شَ	شُ
شَ	شِ	شَ	شَ	شِ
شِ	شَ	شُ	شِ	شَ
شَ	شِ	شِ	شَ	شُ
شِ	شُ	شِ	شَ	شِ
شُ	شِ	شَ	شُ	شَ
شِ	شِ	شُ	شَ	شِ

Read each row from right to left.

صُ	صَ	صُ	صِ	صَ
صَ	صِ	صَ	صُ	صِ
صِ	صَ	صِ	صَ	صُ
صَ	صُ	صِ	صُ	صِ
صِ	صَ	صَ	صُ	صَ
صَ	صِ	صُ	صِ	صُ
صِ	صِ	صَ	صُ	صِ
صَ	صِ	صِ	صُ	صَ

Read each row from right to left.

ضِ	ضِ	ضُ	ضَ	ضُ
ضَ	ضِ	ضِ	ضِ	ضُ
ضَ	ضِ	ضُ	ضِ	ضِ
ضِ	ضُ	ضَ	ضَ	ضُ
ضِ	ضِ	ضُ	ضِ	ضَ
ضِ	ضَ	ضِ	ضُ	ضَ
ضِ	ضُ	ضَ	ضِ	ضُ
ضِ	ضُ	ضِ	ضُ	ضَ

Read each row from right to left.

Read each row from right to left.

ظَ	ظُ	ظِ	ظَ	ظُ	ظَ
ظُ	ظِ	ظُ	ظِ	ظَ	ظُ
ظَ	ظِ	ظِ	ظِ	ظِ	ظِ
ظِ	ظِ	ظَ	ظَ	ظُ	ظِ
ظَ	ظِ	ظُ	ظِ	ظَ	ظِ
ظِ	ظِ	ظُ	ظَ	ظِ	ظُ

Read each row from right to left.

ﻉَ   ﻉُ   ﻉَ   ﻉَ   ﻉَ   ﻉَ
ﻉَ

ﻉَ   ﻉُ   ﻉَ   ﻉَ   ﻉَ   ﻉُ
ﻉُ

ﻉُ   ﻉَ   ﻉَ   ﻉُ   ﻉَ   ﻉَ
ﻉَ

ﻉَ   ﻉَ   ﻉَ   ﻉَ   ﻉَ   ﻉَ
ﻉَ

ﻉَ   ﻉَ   ﻉُ   ﻉَ   ﻉَ
ﻉَ

ﻉُ   ﻉُ   ﻉُ   ﻉَ   ﻉَ
ﻉَ

Read each row from right to left.

غِ غُ غِ غَ غِ غِ غَ

غِ غُ غِ غُ غِ غِ غِ

غِ غَ غَ غُ غِ غِ غُ

غِ غَ غُ غَ غِ غِ غَ

غِ غَ غِ غَ غُ غُ غُ

غِ غُ غَ غِ غِ غِ غَ

Read each row from right to left.

فِ	فَ	فَ	فِ	فُ	فَ
فُ	فِ	فَ	فِ	فَ	فُ
فُ	فَ	فَ	فُ	فَ	فِ
فَ	فِ	فِ	فَ	فِ	فَ
فِ	فِ	فَ	فُ	فَ	فِ
فُ	فُ	فِ	فُ	فَ	فَ
فُ	فَ	فَ	فُ	فَ	فُ

Read each row from right to left.

قَ	قُ	قَ	قِ	قَ	قَ
قِ	قَ	قُ	قُ	قِ	قَ
قُ	قَ	قِ	قُ	قَ	قِ
قَ	قِ	قَ	قَ	قِ	قِ
قُ	قَ	قِ	قِ	قِ	قَ
قُ	قَ	قَ	قُ	قُ	قَ
	قِ				

Read each row from right to left.

كُ	كَ	كَ	كَ	كٍ	كٍ
كَ	كُ	كَ	كٍ	كُ	كٍ
كِ	كِ	كِ	كَ	كُ	كُ
كِ	كَ	كِ	كِ	كَ	كَ
كَ	كِ	كِ	كِ	كِ	كُ
كَ	كَ	كَ	كُ	كَ	كُ

Read each row from right to left.

لَ   لُ   لَ   لَ   لُ   لَ
لِ

لُ   لَ   لَ   لَ   لَ   لُ
لِ

لَ   لَ   لُ   لَ   لَ   لُ
لِ   لِ

لَ   لَ   لَ   لَ   لَ   لَ
لِ   لِ   لِ

لَ   لُ   لَ   لَ   لَ   لَ
لِ   لِ

لَ   لُ   لَ   لُ   لُ   لُ
لِ

Read each row from right to left.

مِ مَ مَ مِ مُ مَ

مُ مَ مَ مِ مَ مُ

مُ مَ مَ مُ مَ مِ

مَ مِ مَ مَ مِ مَ

مِ مَ مِ مُ مَ مِ

مُ مُ مِ مُ مَ مَ

Read each row from right to left.

نَ نِ نَ نَ نِ نُ

نِ نُ نَ نِ نُ نَ

نَ نُ نُ نَ نِ نَ

نِ نَ نَ نِ نَ نِ

نِ نِ نَ نَ نُ نَ

نِ نُ نِ نُ نَ نِ

Read each row from right to left.

Read each row from right to left.

وَ　وُ　وُ　وُ　وِ　وِ

وِ　وُ　وُ　وُ　وِ　وَ

وُ　وِ　وِ　وُ　و　وُ

وُ　وُ　وِ　وُ　و　وَ

وَ　وِ　وِ　وَ　وِ　وَ

وُ　وِ　وِ　وَ　وِ　وُ

وُ　وِ　و　وُ　وِ　وِ

Read each row from right to left.

يَ　يَ　يِ　يِ　يَ　يُؠ

يَ　يَ　يَ　يُؠ　يُؠ　يَ

يِ　يَ　يُؠ　يُؠ　يِ　يَ

يِ　يِ　يَ　يَ　يَ　يِ

يَ　يِ　يُؠ　يِ　يِ　يَ

يِ　يُؠ　يُؠ　يُؠ　يَ　يِ

يَ　يَ　يُؠ　يُؠ　يُؠ　يِ

Short Vowel Exercise 2.1
Read each row from right to left.

سَ زُ ذَ ذُ رُ سَ ضُ ذَ عُ دُ تَ إِ غَ إِ

ثُ بَ أَ تَ خِ حَ دُ جَ زَ أُ فَ أَ فُ إِ

غِ إِ بُ رَ سُ شُ صَ ضِ ذَ فُ بِ

ظُ أَ ظِ إِ ظَ أَ طَ جَ خُ حَ دُ رُ أَ بُ

زَ وِ هُ نَ تِ مَ شُ ثُ صُ ظِ وَ زُ

مَ نِ تُ هُ سَ ذُ ضُ ظُ وَ شُ رُ بَ

سِ شِ صَ ذَ كِ ذَ لُ ضُ كِ زُ رَ كَ زَ

Short Vowel Exercise 2.2

Read each row from right to left.

. . . .

خَ تُ أَ حَ زُ إِ زَ إِ زَ إِ زَ إِ زَ إِ زَ إِ سَ

خَ إِ خُ أَ خَ تَ دُ حِ جَ دُ تَ خُ دَ خَ جَ دَ حَ

خَ تِ دُ بِ إِ تُ دَ خِ دُ تَ دُ خُ جَ حُ دَ خُ

تِ دَ أُ بِ ثُ بَ أَ خِ إِ جُ بِ ثُ دُ

رَ دُ رَ أُ رُ خَ دِ جُ حَ أُ ذَ إِ ذَ إِ ذَ أُ ذَ

إِ أَ جِ بَ ثِ ذِ جَ حَ خُ أَ ذِ ذُ ذَ ذُ تُ

بَ ثُ ذُ بُ إِ رُ أَ رُ أَ رِ إِ دَ دَ جُ حُ

Short Vowel Exercise 2.3

Read each row from right to left.

- -

سُ أَ ذِ سُ ذِ سِ زُ سَ زِ سُ جُ سِ سَ خِ سَ

شَ إِشِ أ شُ أ شَ سُ أ ثُ سُ أ سُ رِ سَ أُ

صَ أُ حَ ثُ دِ سُ ذَ سُ خُ شَ رُ ذِ شُ

صُ رَ شُ سَ ذِ سُ زُ رَ زُ حَ جُ خِ اصَ إِ

سَ صُ رُ أُ صِ أ ذِ صَ ثِ صُ شُ

ضِ إِ ضُ أُ ضِ إِ ضُ صَ سَ سُ ذُ شُ

بُ ثَ زُ رُ ضُ دَ ضُ دُ ضَ دُ ذَ سِ

Short Vowel Exercise 2.4

Read each row from right to left.

طَ إِ طُ أُ طَ أُ طَ إِ ضُ صُ إِ ضَ ذُ ثَ

دَ طَ ذِ ضُ إِ خَ حَ طُ إِ نُ تُ طَ سَ إِ

إِ أُ ظُ أَ ذُ ثِ بَ إِ تَ زِ زُ زَ طِ تُ جَ

ظُ بَ أُ رَ دِ حُ خَ جُ طَ أُ ظَ إِ ظِ أَ ظَ إِ

عَ بُ إِ تُ زُ رَ ذِ عَ جَ دُ حَ زُ رِ شَ

تَ ثُ بَ رُ ذِ عَ إِ عَ جُ عَ حُ عِ خُ

إِ غَ أُ تُ دَ عَ ذُ ضِ سُ رَ ذُ دَ زِ سَ

Short Vowel Exercise 2.5

Read each row from right to left.

قَ زِ ظُ صُ قَ شُ سِ ذُ غُ عَ غِ أَ غَ

جَ دُ حَ خَ تُ أُ قِ بُ ثَ ضَ شُ سَ

خُ غُ قِ تُ عَ قُ غُ قِ بُ لَ رُ زِ قَ

وَ زُ أُ يَ أُ يُ إِ يَ أُ عَ وَ لُ

فُ أُ غَ عُ قَ فِ ذِ أَ ظِ غَ قِ حَ غَ قُ

أَ كُ إِ كِ أَ كُ أَ كِ أُ بَ أَ غَ شِ سَ ثَ

رَ بُ فُ كِ ذَ ضُ صَ شُ سَ رَ كُ

Short Vowel Exercise 2.6

Read each row from right to left.

بُ كَ لَ أَ لُ ءِ لِ أُ لِ أَ لُ أَ ذِ لَ ظُ طَ

زَ كِ رَ زُ لَ ضَ كَ ذِ كُ صَ شُ سَ

غَ عُ لِ قُ فَ ثِ لُ سُ بَ لَ إِ تِ رُ

إِ سُ لُ بُ لَ كُ لَ زَ ظَ طُ جُ دَ حَ خُ

لَ بُ إِ وَ تُ جَ دُ طُ كَ ظِ زَ كَ ظِ

زُ وَ ظُ صَ ثَ شُ مَ تُ نَ هِ وَ زِ

بَ رِ شَ وِ ظُ ضَ ذُ سَ هَ تَ نَ مَ

Short Vowel Exercise 2.7

Read each row from right to left.

دَ ظَ طُ جَ كِ مِ بَ خَ هُ عُ إِ ثَ إِ رَ

يَ مُ إِ لَ خَ رُ ذُ يَ سُ إِ زَ ضُ جَ

بُ يُ إِ تِ عَ هُ يَ وَ غُ ضَ زِ ظِ

إِ أُ تَ بُ تَ اُ ثَ نُ مَ بَ سُ هَ شَ

ظَ وَ زُ يُ رَ ذِ ضَ صَ ثِ تَ ثُ إِ

حُ طِ إِ نَ تُ طُ بُ فَ كَ ذُ ضَ مَ كِ

خَ تِ زَ كُ رَ تَ جَ دُ طِ ذَ ضُ إِ خُ

ARABIC GAME 1

PREPARATION:

Make cards for the letters and each of the three short vowels. For example for the letter Ba you will make a card showing Ba with Fathah, another card for Ba with Dhamma and another of Ba with Kasra. Do this for each letter.

HOW IT'S PLAYED

1. Place all of the cards in a basket and allow one of the students to shake the basket to mix up the cards.
2. Ask a student to blindly pick a random card from the basket. The student must read their card out loud. Copy the card onto the board.
3. Allow the next student to blindly pick another card from the basket and read the first and second card aloud. Copy the second card onto the board next to the first.

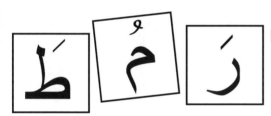

EXAMPLE:

First student: "Ra"
Second student: "Ra" "Mu"
Third student: "Ra" "Mu" "Ta"
Fourth student: "Ra" "Mu" "Ta" "Si"

This game gets more challenging as it progresses and the 'train' of letters on the board gets longer. When a student is unable to read the train of cards they are eliminated from the game. This begins the next round. The student who is able to read the most cards in the train is the winner.

ALTERNATE CLASSROOM RECOMMENDATION:

1. Select one student to shake the basket and pick cards out of the basket. You write the card on the board. The class repeats after you or you select students to read the board.

HOME VERSION:

Lay the cards next to each other on a tabletop or on the floor. As cards are read use them to form a long train.

Write the sound.

	قِ		شَ	Sha
	كَ		ظِ	
	بِ		سُ	
	رُ		زَ	
	فِ		تُ	
	دَ		غَ	
	جَ		لِ	
	حِ		ذُ	
	قُ		صَ	

Section 3: The Long Vowels

In This Section
- Introduction to the long vowels
- Combining the letters with long vowel sounds
- Introduction to the Arabic mark 'Sukun'
- Reading Practice
- Knowledge Self Test

 We will take our next step in reading by working with the letters in combination with long vowels.

Sukun

Sukun is a mark that is written as a circle above the letter. When a letter has the sukun over it this means it makes no vowel sound.

‒‒‒‒‒ *Sukun*

Let's see some examples of the sukun in action.

1.

غْ بِ = غْ بِ
Big   **g**   **Bi**

2.

غْ بَ = غْ بَ
Bag   **g**   **Ba**

Do any of these sound familiar?

3.

نْ رُ = نْ رُ
Run   **n**   **Ru**

4.

تْ سِ = تْ سِ
Sit   **t**   **Si**

Alif is a long vowel that produces a long 'aa' sound. When Alif follows a letter that carries fat-hah it is long vowel Alif. The effect of long vowel Alif is like lengthening fat-hah.

Long aa = ١

What happens when we combine the sound of the letters with the long vowel Alif?

بَـا = ا بَ

	Baa		**aa**	**Ba**

Maa	مَـا	Laa	لَـا
Thaa	ثَـا	Baa	بَـا
Raa	رَـا	Khaa	خَـا
haa	هَـا	Zaa	زَـا
Saa	سَـا	Jaa	جَـا
Naa	نَـا	Faa	فَـا
Ya	يَـا	Daa	ضَـا

A: When Alif follows a letter that carries fat-ha it is long Alif.

Ya is a long vowel that produces a long 'ee' sound. When Ya carries sukun *and* follows a letter that carries kasra it is long vowel Ya. The effect of long vowel Ya is like lengthening kasra.

Long ee = ي

What happens when we combine the sound of the letters with the long vowel Ya?

بِـْي = يْ بِ

Bee   **ee**   **Bi**

Mee	مِـْي		Jee	جِـْي
Tee	تِـْي		See	سِـْي
Bee	بِـْي		Zee	زِـْي
hee	هِـْي		Nee	نِـْي
Shee	شِـْي		Fee	فِـْي
Thee	ثِـْي		Yee	يِـْي
Gee	غِـْي		Ree	رِـْي

A: When ya carries sukun and follows a letter that carries kasra it becomes long Ya.

Waw is a long vowel that produces a long 'oo' sound. When waw carries sukun **and** follows a letter that carries damma it is long vowel Waw. The effect of long vowel Waw is like lengthening damma.

Long oo = و

What happens when we combine the sound of the letters with the long vowel Waw?

بُوْ = وْ بُ

Boo   **oo**   **Bu**

Doo	ضُوْ	Loo	لُوْ	
Thoo	ثُوْ	Boo	بُوْ	
Roo	رُوْ	Khoo	خُوْ	
Woo	وُوْ	Zoo	زُوْ	
Moo	مُوْ	Joo	جُوْ	
Shoo	شُوْ	Yoo	يُوْ	
Too	تُوْ	Soo	سُوْ	

A: When waw carries sukun and follows a letter that carries damma it is long waw.

Read each row from right to left.

أُوْ   اَا   إِيْ   اَا   أَوْ

أُوْ   إِيْ   اَا   أُوْ   إِيْ   إِيْ

اَا   إِيْ   إِيْ   اَا   أَوْ   إِيْ

إِيْ   اَا   أَا   إِيْ   أُوْ   اَا   أَا

أُوْ   اَا   أَا   إِيْ   أُوْ   إِيْ   أُوْ

إِيْ   إِيْ   اَا   أُوْ   أَا   أُوْ   إِيْ

أَا   إِيْ   أُوْ   إِيْ   اَا   أُوْ

Read each row from right to left.

بُوْ بِيْ بَا بِيْ بَا بِيْ بِيْ

بِيْ بُوْ بِيْ بُوْ بُوْ بِيْ بِيْ

بُوْ بَا بِيْ بُوْ بَا بُوْ بِيْ بَا

بَا بَا بُوْ بَا بُوْ بَا بُوْ بُوْ

بِيْ بِيْ بَا بِيْ بَا بَا بِيْ

بِيْ بَا بِيْ بُوْ بِيْ بَا بِيْ بِيْ

بَا بُوْ بِيْ بَا بِيْ بُوْ بَا

بُوْ بِيْ بُوْ بَا بُوْ بَا

Read each row from right to left.

تِيْ تَا ثُوْ تِيْ تُوْ تَا ثُوْ تَا

ثُوْ تَا تِيْ ثُوْ تَا ثُوْ تَا ثَا

ثَا تِيْ ثُوْ تِيْ ثَا تَا ثَا ثَا

ثُوْ تَا ثَا ثُوْ تِيْ تِيْ ثُوْ

ثَا تِيْ ثُوْ تَا ثَا تِيْ تِيْ تِيْ

تِيْ تِيْ تِيْ تَا ثُوْ تَا ثُوْ ثَا

ثُوْ تِيْ تِيْ ثُوْ تِيْ ثُوْ

ثُوْ تِيْ تَا ثُوْ تَا تِيْ ثَا

Read each row from right to left.

ثَا ثِي ثَا ثُوْ ثَا ثِي ثُوْ ثَا

ثُوْ ثِي ثَا ثُوْ ثَا ثِي ثُوْ ثَا

ثُوْ ثِي ثَا ثُوْ ثِي ثَا ثِي ثُوْ

ثَا ثِي ثُوْ ثَا ثُوْ ثِي ثِي ثُوْ

ثُوْ ثِي ثَا ثُوْ ثَا ثِي ثَا ثِي

ثِي ثُوْ ثِي ثَا ثِي ثُوْ ثِي ثَا

ثَا ثِي ثَا ثُوْ ثَا ثُوْ ثِي ثَا

ثِي ثُوْ ثَا ثُوْ ثِي ثَا ثِي ثَا

Read each row from right to left.

جِي	جَا	جِي	جَا	جُو	جَا
جُو	جِي	جِي	جُو	جَا	جِي
جَا	جَا	جُو	جِي	جَا	جُو
جِي	جُو	جَا	جَا	جُو	جَا
جُو	جَا	جِي	جَا	جِي	جُو
جُو	جِي	جُو	جِي	جِي	جُو
جِي	جَا	جِي	جَا	جُو	جَا

Read each row from right to left.

حَا حِيْ حَ حَا حِيْ حُوْ حَا

حِيْ حَا حَا حِيْ حَ حُوْ حِيْ

حَا حَا حِيْ حَ حُوْ حُوْ حُوْ

حِيْ حُوْ حِيْ حُوْ حِيْ حَا حَا

حَا حَا حُوْ حِيْ حَ حُوْ حِيْ

حِيْ حَا حَا حِيْ حُوْ حِيْ حَا

حَا حَا حِيْ حَا حَا حِيْ حُوْ

Read each row from right to left.

خُوْ خَا خُوْ خُوْ خَا خُوْ

خِيْ خُوْ خُوْ خَا خِيْ

خُوْ خَا خُوْ خُوْ خِيْ خَا

خَا خِيْ خِيْ خُوْ خِيْ خُوْ

خِيْ خِيْ خُوْ خِيْ خَا خَا

خَا خُوْ خِيْ خَا خَا خِيْ

خُوْ خَا خِيْ خُوْ خُوْ

Read each row from right to left.

دَا	دُوْ	دَا	دَا	دِيْ
دِيْ	دَا	دِيْ	دُوْ	دِيْ
دُوْ	دُوْ	دَا	دِيْ	دَا
دِيْ	دِيْ	دُوْ	دِيْ	دَا
دِيْ	دَا	دُوْ	دَا	دُوْ
دَا	دِيْ	دَا	دُوْ	دِيْ
دِيْ	دَا	دُوْ	دِيْ	دَا
دَا	دُوْ	دُوْ	دَا	دُوْ

Read each row from right to left.

ذَا	ذِي	ذَا	ذُوْ	ذَا
ذَا	ذِيْ	ذِيْ	ذَا	ذِيْ
ذُوْ	ذَا	ذُوْ	ذِيْ	ذُوْ
ذَا	ذِيْ	ذَا	ذُوْ	ذَا
ذَا	ذُوْ	ذِيْ	ذُوْ	ذِيْ
ذِيْ	ذِيْ	ذُوْ	ذِيْ	ذُوْ
ذُوْ	ذُوْ	ذِيْ	ذَا	ذِيْ
ذُوْ	ذَا	ذَا	ذُوْ	ذَا

Read each row from right to left.

رَا	رُوْ	رَا	رِيْ رِيْ		رِيْ
رِيْ	رَا	رِيْ	رَا		رُوْ
رَا	رِيْ	رُوْ	رِيْ		رَا
رُوْ	رَا	رَا	رِيْ		رُوْ
رِيْ	رِيْ	رُوْ	رَا		رِيْ
رَا	رِيْ	رِيْ	رُوْ		رَا
رِيْ	رِيْ	رَا	رِيْ		رُوْ
رُوْ	رَا	رُوْ	رُوْ		رَا

Read each row from right to left.

زِيْ زَا زِيْ زَا زُوْ زُا زُوْ زُوْ

زُوْ زُوْ زَا زِيْ زَا زُوْ زُوْ زِيْ

زَا زِيْ زُوْ زِيْ زُوْ زَا زِيْ زُوْ

زِيْ زَا زَا زُوْ زُوْ زُوْ زُوْ زِيْ

زُوْ زَا زِيْ زَا زُوْ زِيْ زُوْ زُوْ

زُوْ زَا زُوْ زِيْ زُوْ زِيْ زُوْ

زَا زِيْ زُوْ زَا زِيْ زَا زَا

زِيْ زَا زِيْ زَا زِيْ زَا زَا

Read each row from right to left.

سَا سِيْ سَا سُوْ سَا سُوْ سُيْ سِي

سِيْ سَا سِيْ سَا سُوْ سَا سُوْ

سِيْ سَا سِوْ سِيْ سَا سِيْ سَا

سِيْ سَا سُوْ سِيْ سُوْ سَا سُوْ

سَا سَا سِيْ سَا سُوْ سُيْ سِيْ

سُوْ سِيْ سُيْ سَا سِيْ سِوْ سُوْ

سَا سُوْ سِيْ سَا سُوْ سَا

Read each row from right to left.

شَا	شَا	شُوْ	شَا	شُوْ
شَا	شِيْ	شَا	شَا	شِيْ
شِيْ	شَا	شُوْ	شِيْ	شَا
شَا	شِيْ	شِيْ	شَا	شُوْ
شِيْ	شُوْ	شِيْ	شُوْ	شِيْ
شُوْ	شِيْ	شَا	شُوْ	شَا
شِيْ	شِيْ	شُوْ	شَا	شِيْ

Read each row from right to left.

صُوْ صَا صُوْ صِيْ صَا

صَا صِيْ صَوْ صُوْ صِيْ

صِيْ صَا صِيْ صَوْ صُوْ

صَا صُوْ صِيْ صُوْ صِيْ

صِيْ صَا صَوْ صُوْ صَا

صَا صِيْ صُوْ صِيْ صُوْ

صِيْ صِيْ صَا صُوْ صِيْ

صَا صِيْ صُوْ صَا

Read each row from right to left.

ضَا ضَا ضُوْ ضِيْ ضَيْ

ضُوْ ضَا ضَيْ ضِيْ ضَيْ ضَا

ضَا ضِيْ ضُوْ ضَيْ ضَيْ ضَا

ضُوْ ضَا ضَا ضُوْ ضِيْ

ضَا ضِيْ ضُوْ ضَيْ ضِيْ ضَيْ

ضَا ضُوْ ضِيْ ضَيْ ضَا ضَا

ضُوْ ضَيْ ضَا ضُوْ ضِيْ

ضَا ضُوْ ضِيْ ضُوْ ضِيْ

Read each row from right to left.

طَا   طِيْ   طِيْ   طُوْ   طِيْ   طِيْ

طِيْ   طُوْ   طَا   طِيْ   طُوْ   طَا

طُوْ   طَا   طُوْ   طَا   طَا   طَا

طَا   طِيْ   طَا   طِيْ   طَا   طَا

طِيْ   طُوْ   طِيْ   طُوْ   طَا   طُوْ

طَا   طِيْ   طُوْ   طِيْ   طِيْ   طِيْ

طِيْ   طُوْ   طِيْ   طُوْ   طَا   طُوْ

Read each row from right to left.

ظِي ظُو ظَا ظِي ظُو ظَا

ظُو ظِي ظُو ظَا ظِي ظَا ظُو

ظَا ظَا ظِي ظَا ظَا ظِي ظِي

ظِي ظِي ظَا ظَا ظُو ظَا ظَا

ظَا ظِي ظُو ظَا ظِي ظَا ظِي

ظِي ظِي ظَا ظُو ظِي ظَا ظُو

ظِي ظَا ظُو ظِي ظَا ظُو ظَا

Read each row from right to left.

اَ عُوْ عِيْ اَ اَ عِيْ

عُوْ عِيْ عَا عِيْ عَا عُوْ

عِيْ اَ عُوْ اَ عِيْ عِيْ

اَ عِيْ عَا عِيْ عِيْ اَ

عِيْ عِيْ اَ عُوْ عَا عِيْ

عُوْ عُوْ عِيْ عُوْ عِيْ اَ

عُوْ اَ اَ عُوْ عِيْ عُوْ

Read each row from right to left.

غُوْ غَا غْي غَا غِي غَا غْي غَا

غَا غِي غَا غْي غُوْ غْي غَا غِي

غِي غَا غْي غُوْ غَا غُوْ غِي غْوُ

غَا غْي غِي غَا غُوْ غُوْ غْي غَا

غُوْ غُوْ غْي غِي غَا غْي غْي غُوْ

غَا غْي غِي غَا غُوْ غَا غْي غَا

غُوْ غُوْ غُوْ غُوْ غَا غُوْ غَا

Read each row from right to left.

فِيْ فَا فَا فُوْ فِيْ فَا

فُوْ فَا فِيْ فَا فِيْ فُوْ

فِيْ فَا فُوْ فِيْ فَا فُوْ

فَا فِيْ فَا فِيْ فِيْ فَا

فِيْ فَا فُوْ فَا فِيْ فِيْ

فَا فِيْ فُوْ فِيْ فُوْ فُوْ

فُوْ فِيْ فُوْ فَا فَا فُوْ

Read each row from right to left.

قَا قَا قِيْ قَا قِيْ قِيْ

قَا قِيْ قُوْ قُوْ قِيْ قِيْ

قِيْ قَا قِيْ قُوْ قَا قُوْ

قِيْ قِيْ قَا قَا قِيْ قَا

قَا قِيْ قِيْ قَا قَا قُوْ

قِيْ قُوْ قَا قُوْ قِيْ قُوْ

قَا قَا قُوْ قُوْ قِيْ قُوْ

Read each row from right to left.

كُوْ اكَ اكَ كِيْ كَا كَا كِيْ

كَا كَا كُوْ كِيْ كُوْ كَا كِيْ

كَا كِيْ كِيْ كَا كُوْ كُوْ كُوْ

لِكِيْ كَا كِيْ كِيْ كَا كَا كَا

كَا كِيْ كِيْ كَا كِيْ كُوْ كُوْ

كِيْ كَا كُوْ كَا كَا كِيْ كُوْ

كُوْ كِيْ كَا كُوْ كُوْ كُوْ

Read each row from right to left.

لَ ا لُ وْ لِ يْ لَ ا لَ ا لِ يْ

لُ وْ لَ ا لِ يْ لَ ا لِ يْ لُ وْ

لِ يْ لَ ا لُ وْ لِ يْ لَ ا لُ وْ

لَ ا لِ يْ لَ ا لِ يْ لِ يْ لَ ا

لِ يْ لَ ا لُ وْ لَ ا لِ يْ لِ يْ

لَ ا لِ يْ لُ وْ لِ يْ لُ وْ لُ وْ

لُ وْ لَ ا لَ ا لُ وْ لِ يْ لُ وْ

Read each row from right to left.

مَا	مُو	مِي	اَ	مَ اَ	مِ	مِي	
مُو	مَ اَ	مِي	اَ مَ	مُو	اَمَ	مِي	مُو
مِي	اَمَ	مُو	مِي	اَ مَ	مِي	اَمَ	مُو
اَمَ	مِي	مِي	اَمَ	مِي	اَمَ	مِي	
مِي	مُو	اَمَ	اَمَ	مِي	مِي	مِي	
اَمَ	مِي	مُو	مُو	مُو	مِي	مُو	
مُو	اَمَ	اَمَ	مُو	مِي	مُو		

Read each row from right to left.

نَا نِيْ نَا نِيْ نَا نُوْ

نِيْ نُوْ نَا نِيْ نُوْ نَا

نَا نُوْ نِيْ نُوْ نِيْ نَا

نِيْ نَا نِيْ نَا نَا نِيْ

نِيْ نِيْ نَا نُوْ نِيْ نَا

نُوْ نِيْ نُوْ نَا نُوْ نِيْ

نِيْ نُوْ نَا نُوْ نُوْ نِيْ

Read each row from right to left.

هَا   هَا   هِيْ   هُوْ   هَا

هِيْ   هِيْ   هُوْ   هَا   هِيْ

هِيْ   هِيْ   هُوْ   هُوْ   هَا

هُوْ   هُوْ   هِيْ   هَا   هِيْ

هُوْ   هِيْ   هَا   هِيْ   هُوْ

هُوْ   هِيْ   هِيْ   هَا   هِيْ

هُوْ   هَا   هَا   هُوْ   هِيْ

Read each row from right to left.

وِيْ	وِيْ	وِيْ	وَا	وُوْ	وَا	وِيْ
وِيْ	وَا	وَا	وِيْ	وُوْ	وَا	وَا
وُوْ	وَا	وَا	وُوْ	وِيْ	وُوْ	وُوْ
وُوْ	وُوْ	وِيْ	وُوْ	وِيْ	وَا	وَا
وَا	وِيْ	وِيْ	وَا	وِيْ	وَا	وَا
وُوْ	وِيْ	وَا	وِيْ	وَا	وُوْ	وُوْ
وُوْ	وَا	وِيْ	وُوْ	وَا	وِيْ	وِيْ

Read each row from right to left.

يَا   يَٱ   اَيْ   يِيْ   يِيْ   يَٱ   يُوْ

يَٱ   يَا   يُوْ   يُوْ   يِيْ   يِيْ   يَٱ

يِيْ   يَٱ   يُوْ   يُوْ   يَٱ   يِيْ   يَٱ

يِيْ   يِيْ   يَٱ   يَٱ   يِيْ   يَٱ   يِيْ

يَٱ   يِيْ   يِيْ   يُوْ   يِيْ   يِيْ   يَٱ

يِيْ   يَٱ   يُوْ   يُوْ   يُوْ   يِيْ   يِيْ

يَٱ   يُوْ   يُوْ   يَٱ   يُوْ   يِيْ   يِيْ

Mixed Practice Exercise 3.1
Read each row from right to left.

زَا   رِي   ذُو   دَا   اغَ

بَا   اخَ   دُو   وَا   يَا

رِي   سُو   شُو   بِي

ظَا   ذَا   جَ   دُو   بَا

صَا   كِي   زِي   كَا

قَا   حَ   قُو   بِي

Mixed Practice Exercise 3.2
Read each row from right to left.

خِيْ	زِيْ	تُوْ	سُوْ
اخَ	تَا	دَ	حِيْ
تُوْ	دَا	جُوْ	دَا
ثِيْ	بَا	تُوْ	دِيْ
رِيْ	خُوْ	حَا	سُوْ
جَا	ذَا	ذِا	تَا
ذُوْ	جَا	رُوْ	حَا
سَا	رِيْ	دِيْ	خَا

Mixed Practice Exercise 3.3
Read each row from right to left.

خَا ذِي زِيْ سُوْ زِيْ اِ سَا

سَا ثُوْ شَا وِيْ شَا اِ شَا

خَا حَا رِيْ ذِي ذِي صُوْ

صُوْ ذَا صَا سُوْ

ضَا صَا سُوْ ذُوْ

ذِي دِيْ زُوْ بَا

Mixed Practice Exercise 3.4
Read each row from right to left.

ذَا	صَا	نَا	تِيْ		
حُوْ	طَا	خِيْ	ذَا		
سَا	ثُوْ	بَا	زُوْ	تُوْ	
ظَا	رِيْ	جَا	ظَا	ظَا	
بِيْ	تُوْ	رُوْ	شَا		
تَا	بِيْ	ذُوْ	طَا		

Mixed Practice Exercise 3.5
Read each row from right to left.

غِيْ	سُوْ	قَا	قِيْ		
شُوْ	ثَا	قَا	حَا	جَا	
لِيْ	بُوْ	قَا	قُوْ		
لُوْ	يَا	فِيْ	زُوْ		
حَا	ظَا	قِيْ	ذَا		
سَا	أَغْ	شَا	كَا		

Mixed Practice Exercise 3.6
Read each row from right to left.

حُوْ	مِيْ	هَـا	نِيْ	مِيْ
رِيْ	حُوْ	بَـا	جُوْ	حُوْ
سَـا	جَ	صُوْ		جَ
حِيْ	سِيْ	بَـا	حَا	سِيْ
كِيْ	فَـا	نَـا	كِيْ	كِيْ
بَـا	بَـا	قَـا	بِيْ	بَـا

Write the sound.

	قِ شْ		بَ ظْ
		Baz	

	كَ بْ		سُ بْ

	بِ لْ		زُ بْ

	رَ ثْ		زُ قْ

	تَ بْ		تَ لْ

	دَ فْ		غَ رْ

	جَ بْ		لَ ا

	حَ تْ		ذَ سْ

	قُ لْ		صَ ا

Write the sound.

	ح اَ		بِ يْ
		Bee	
	لُ وْ		زُ وْ
	زِ يْ		قَ ا
	ثُ وْ		صُ وْ
	تِ يْ		فَ ا
	دَ ا		غِ يْ
	جِ يْ		شَ ا
	قُ وْ		كُ وْ
	ظَ ا		سَ ا

Section 4: Steps in Reading

- -

In This Section
▶ Reading groups of letters with short and long vowels
▶ Reading Practice
▶ Fluency Activity
▶ Knowledge Self Test

- -

 We will begin taking steps in reading. We are now ready to tackle groups of letters.

Steps in Reading Exercise 4.1

Read each row from right to left.

زَس   رُذِ   ذُسُ   دِع   غْب

أَبُ   خَت   دُحَ   زَا   إفْ

رُغِ   سْب   شُذِ   بِف

ظُأَ   ظُإِ   ظَا   جَ ا   دُحْ   بُأَ

صِس   كْذ   زِلُ   كَرُ

قَا   إقْ   قُلْ   بَعْ

Steps in Reading Exercise 4.2

Read each row from right to left.

....

خِتُ	دِزُ	تُزَ	سُزِ
خِرَ	دَتُ	دَخُ	حُجِ
دُتُ	دَتِ	جُدَ	دَحَ
ثِدَ	بَثِ	تُخَ	دِدَ
رِدُ	خُحُ	حَجُ	ذُسِ
جَرَ	ذَثِ	ذِحَ	تَذُ
ذُثِ	جِثَ	دُرِ	حَجَ
سَذَ	رِسَ	دِذَ	خُحَ

....

Steps in Reading Exercise 4.3

Read each row from right to left.

خْ سَ جُ زِ سُ ذِ سُرْ

سَ ا ثَ سُ شَ نْ إِ شَ

خِ ا حَ رُ ذِ نْ رَ صُ

صُ شْ إِ ذَ إِ صَ رُ سَ

ذُ شْ سُ إِ ذُ صَ ا ضَ

ذِ سْ دَ دْ زُ ثَ بَ

Steps in Reading Exercise 4.4

Read each row from right to left.

تِدُ   طَنَ   صَا   إِذْ

ذَا   خَحَ   طْسْ

ذُثِ   بِأَ   زُتْ   تُجَ

ظُبَ   رُدْ   جُأَ   ظِإ   ظَا

عَبْ   تُزُ   ذِجَ   دُحَ   رِش

تَثُ   بُرَ   ذِعَ   إِجُ

Steps in Reading Exercise 4.5

Read each row from right to left.

ذَ غِ سُ قُشُ سُغ قِزُ

جَ دُ شُسَ ثَ بَ أَقْ حَتَ

لِقَ بُرَ قُثُ عَقْ

زُوْ فُيَ ذَتْ وَلَ

هَ ذَ قِفْ ظَا حَقُ

نَثْ سَثْ شِمْ غَا

Steps in Reading Exercise 4.6

Read each row from right to left.

not

them (m)　　　　　　not (future tense)　　　　　no

Did you tackle these without any trouble?
Yes. Congratulations!
No. If you had trouble pinpoint whether it was with letter recognition or the vowels and review the pratice exercises before going on.

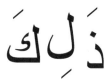

he　　　　　　not (past tense)　　　　　that

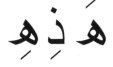 

these (f)　　　　　　besides, less than

those(f)　　　　　　she

 نَحْنُ

not　　　　　　we

ARABIC GAME 2

This activity builds fluency by reinforcing the sounds of Arabic letters and vowels while allowing students to read words they are familiar with.

Read the following English words that have been written using Arabic script.

This reads: Arabic is easy

PREPARATION:

Introduce this method using simple words such as "bag".
This would be written as "Ba with fathah - Gein with sukun"
Refer to the lesson on Sukun in Section 3 for more examples.

HOW IT'S PLAYED

Write a simple word on the board and ask students to "decode" it.

Extension Activities:

▶ For more advanced students you may construct entire English sentences in Arabic script for students to decode. Such as "What do cows eat?" The students who can decode the question will give the correct answer.

▶ Ask students to arrange the cards from the previous activity to form their own words or sentences.

Note: Remind students to always orient words and sentences beginning on the right side. It is crucial that students become comfortable with the right to left orientation of Arabic script.

Name the letter.

	شِ بْ
	جَ بِ
	ثِ يْ
	قَ تْ
	لُ وْ
	حَ بِ
	قَ تُ
	بَ كْ
	فُ سَ ا

Siza	سِ ظَ
	قُ بْ
	بُ زُ
	غُ لَ
	سَ بُ
	رَ زِ
	تَ ا
	عَ شَ رْ
	صَ ا

Section 5 : Writing Arabic Letters

•••

In This Section
▶ Method of writing the letters
▶ Guided Practice Exercises
▶ Independent Practice

•••

 Let's write the Arabic letters.

Lesson: 1

How to write it:
Begin at the top. Complete the letter in a single downward stroke.

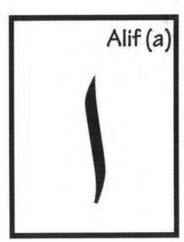

Alif (a)

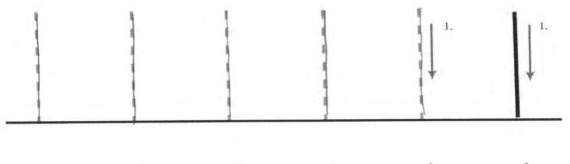

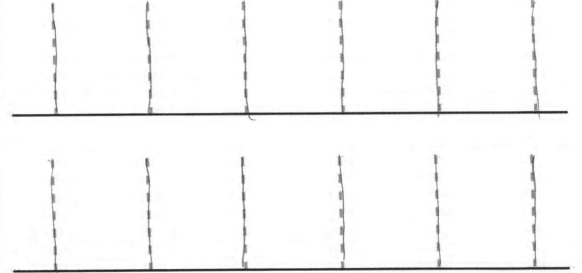

1.

1.

Lesson: 2

How to write it:
Begin at the right tip of the letter. Follow the arrows down, across to the left, and back up. Finish with one dot centered under the letter.

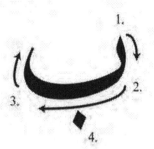

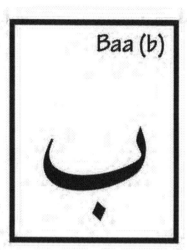

Baa (b)

ب

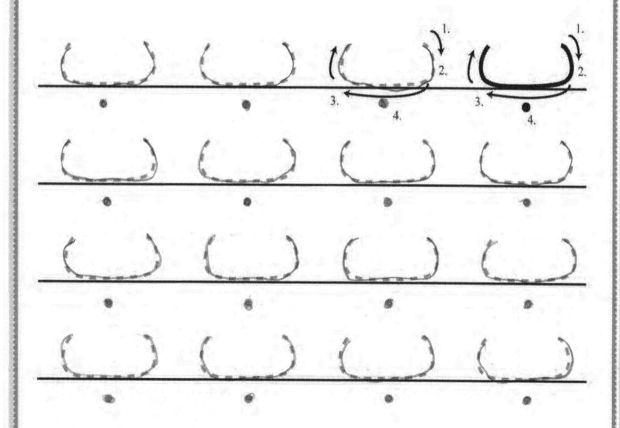

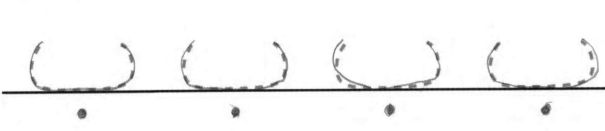

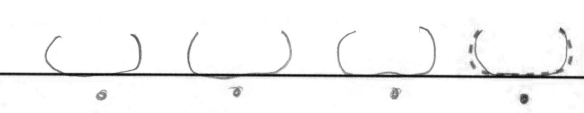

Lesson: 3

How to write it:
Begin at the right tip of the letter. Follow the arrows down, across to the left, and back up. Finish with two dots above the letter.

Taa (t)

ت

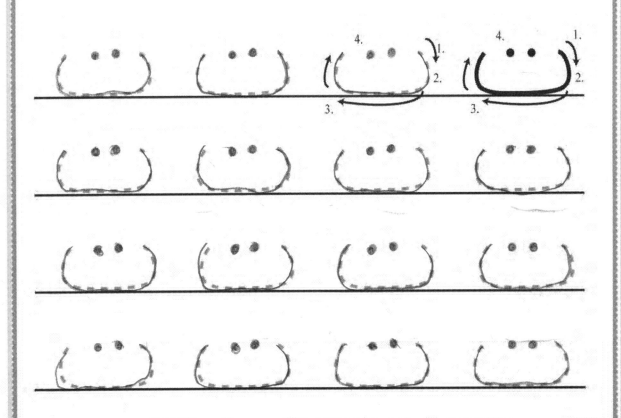

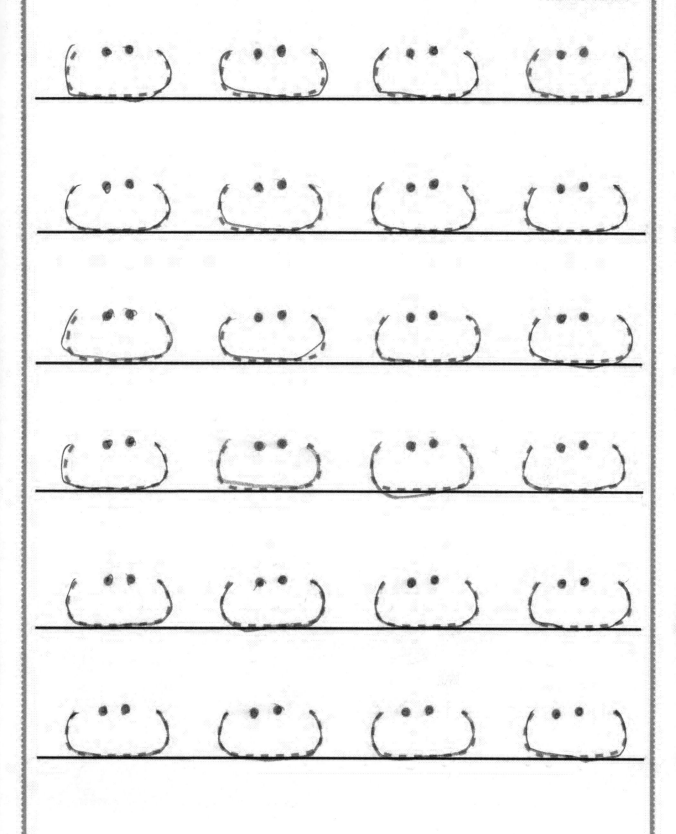

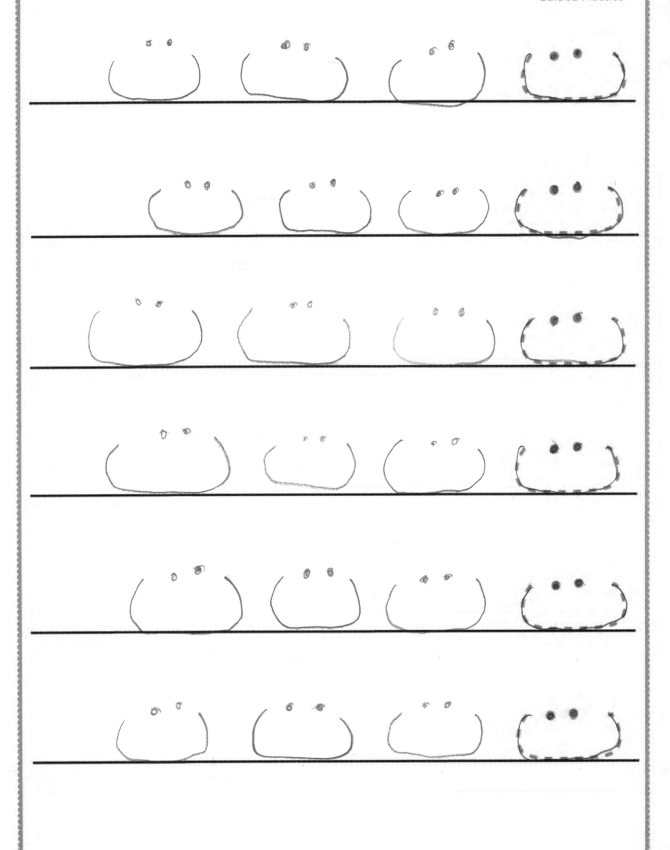

Lesson: 4

How to write it:
Begin at the right tip of the letter. Follow the arrows down, across to the left, and back up. Finish with three dots above the letter.

Thaa (th)

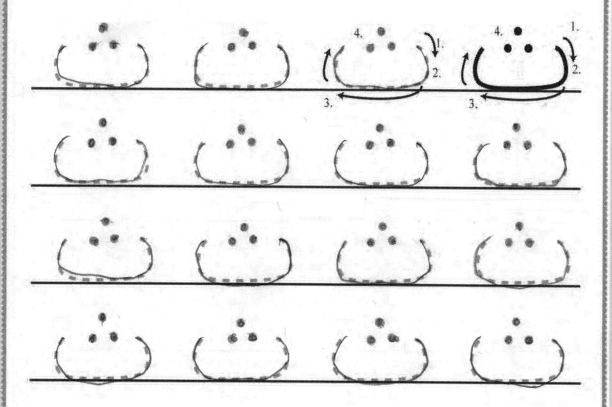

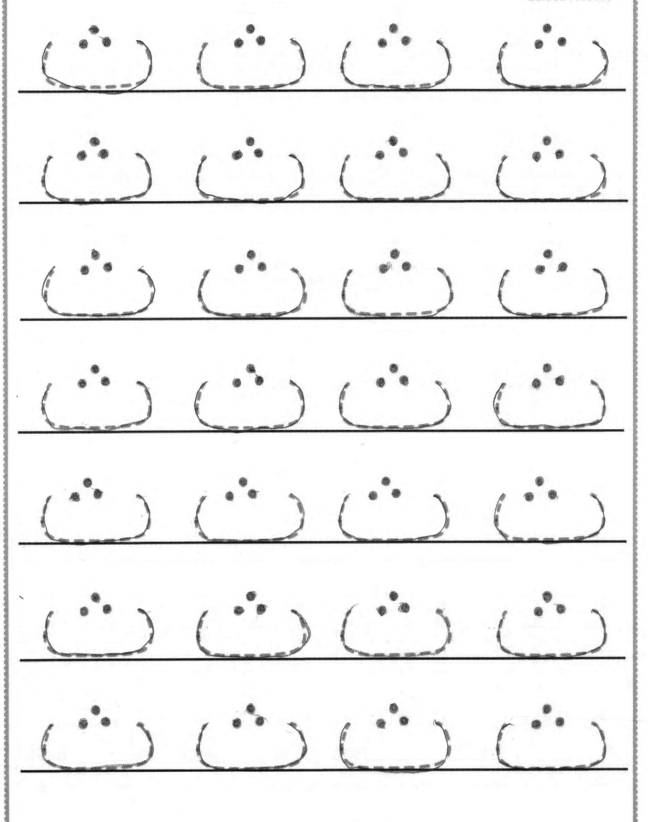

Lesson: 5

How to write it:

Most of this letter lies under the line. Begin at the left and follow the arrow across to the right. Now curve down and around the tail end. Draw a dot inside the curve.

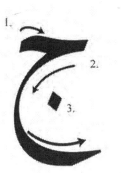

Jeem (j)

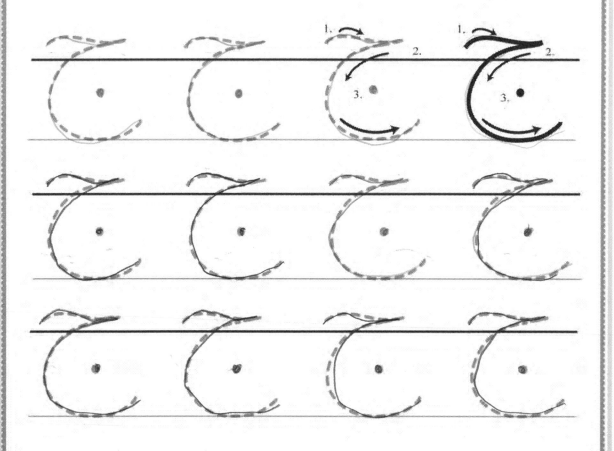

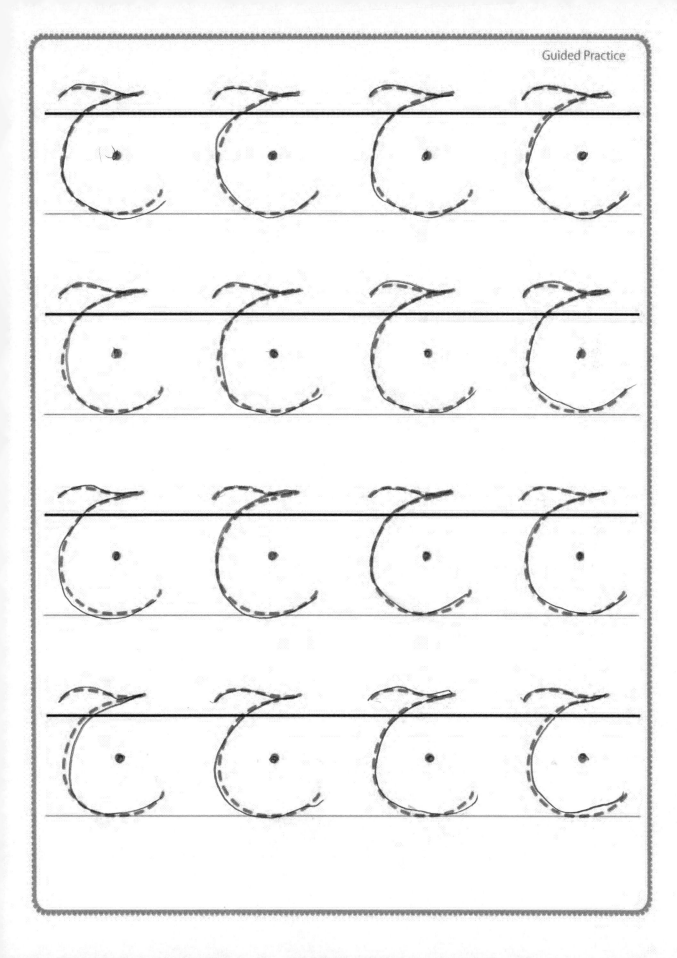

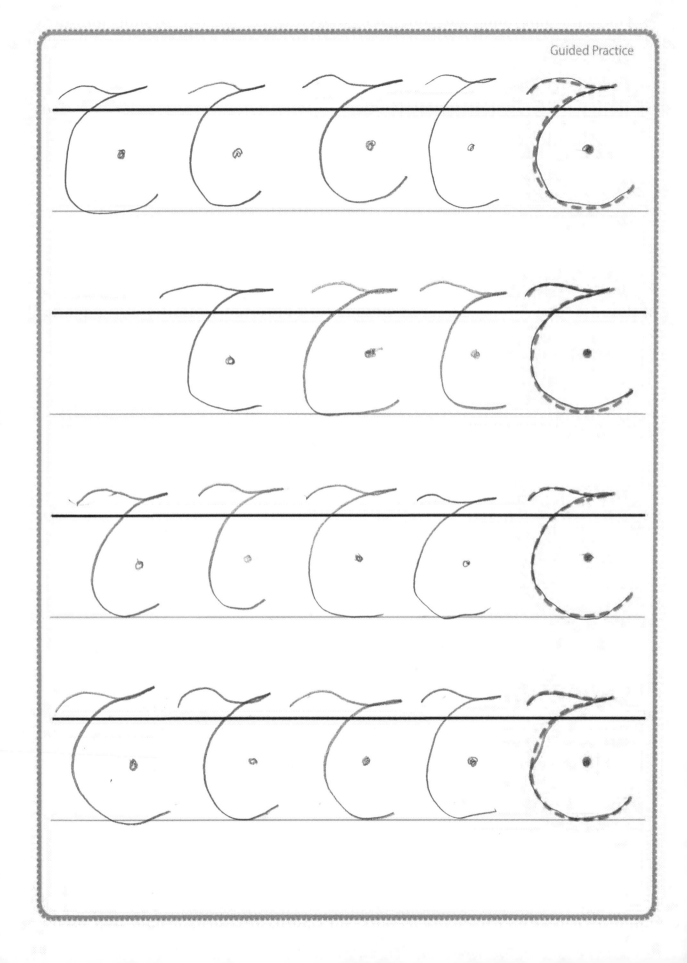

Lesson: 6

How to write it:

Most of this letter lies under the line. Begin at the left and follow the arrow across to the right. Now curve down and around the tail end.

Haa (H)

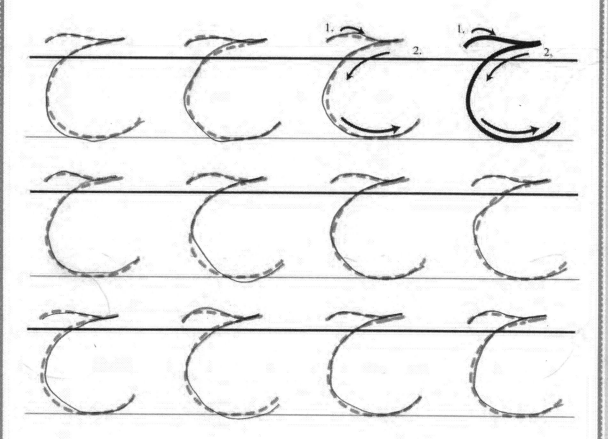

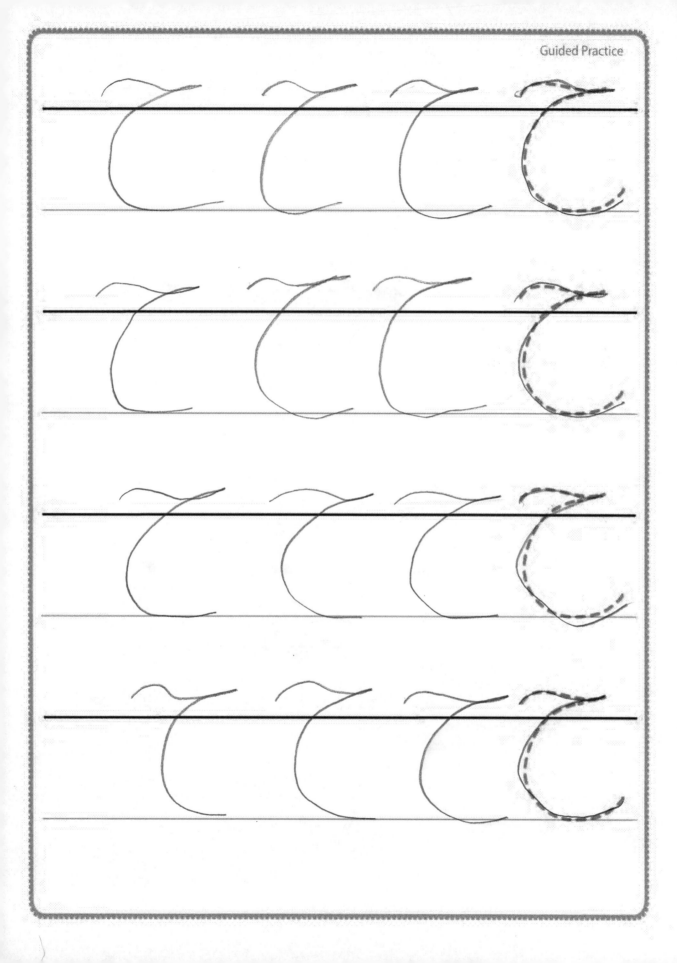

Lesson: 7

How to write it:
Most of this letter lies under the line. Begin at the left and follow the arrow across to the right. Now curve down and around the tail end. Draw a dot above the letter.

Kha (kh)

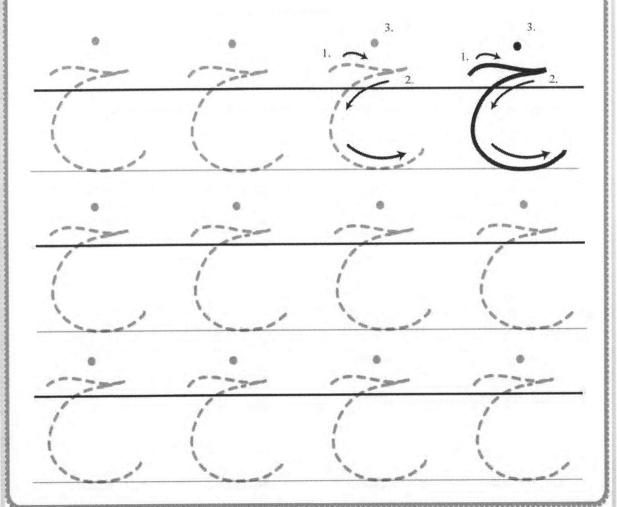

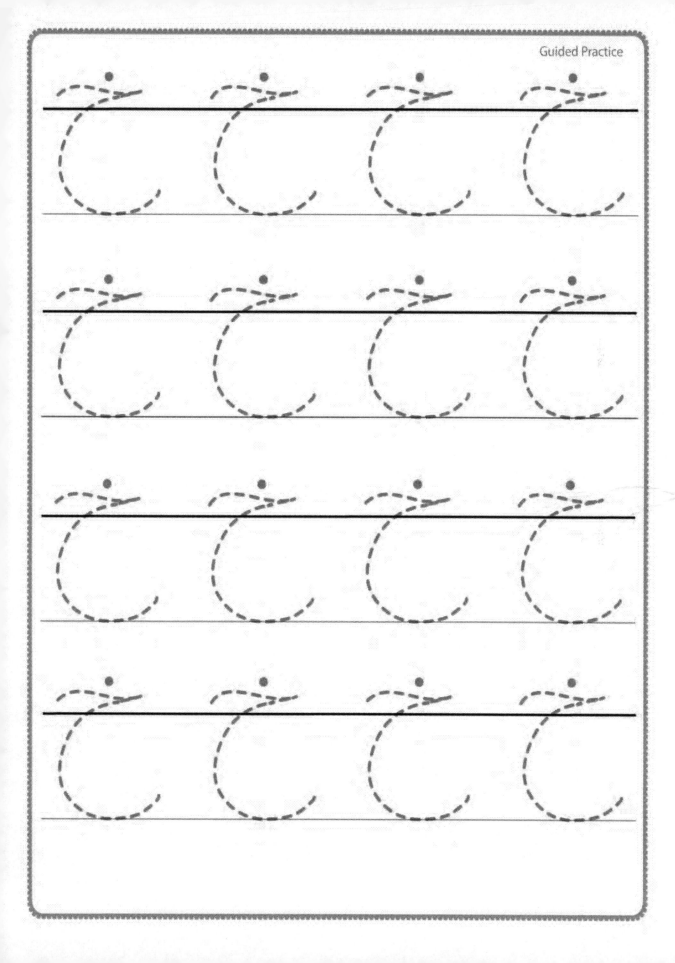

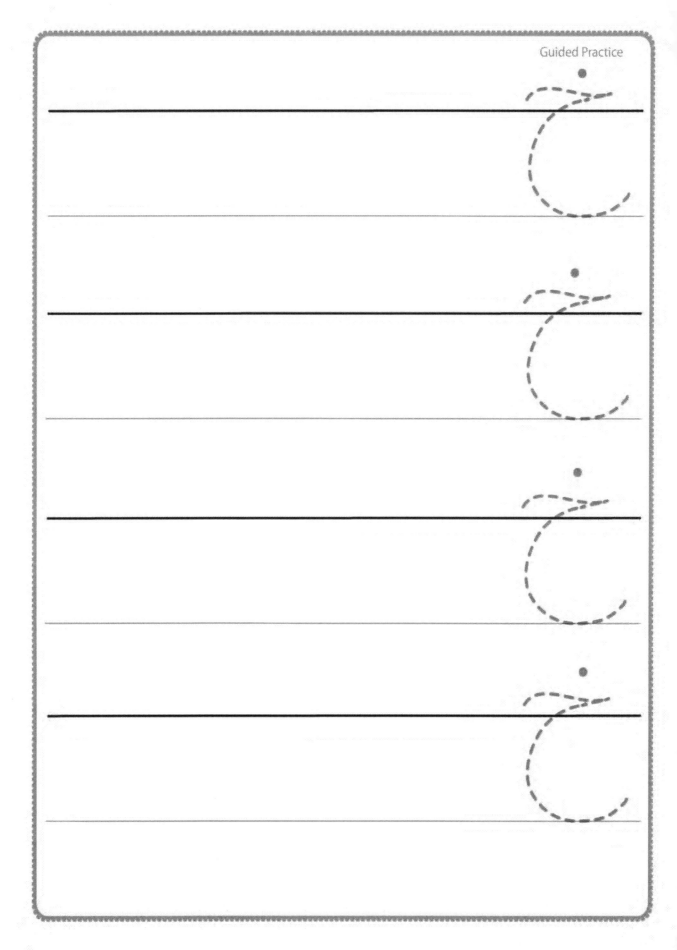

How to write it:
Begin at the top of the letter. Follow the arrow down to the right and across the bottom ending on the left.

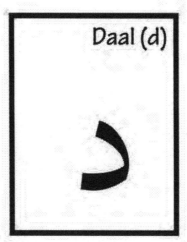

Daal (d)

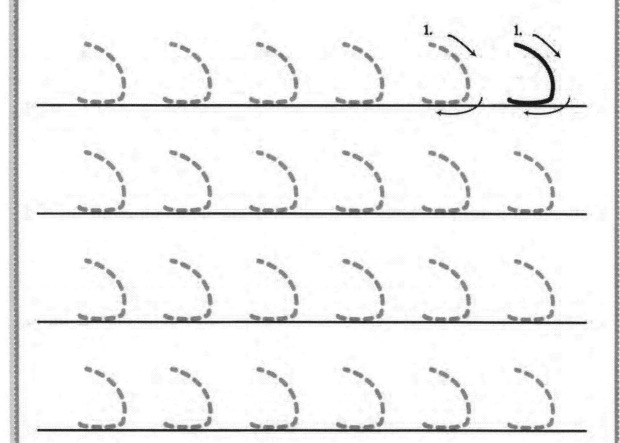

Lesson: 9

How to write it:
Begin at the top of the letter. Follow the arrow down to the right and across the bottom ending on the left. Finish with one dot above the letter.

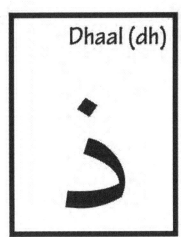

Dhaal (dh)

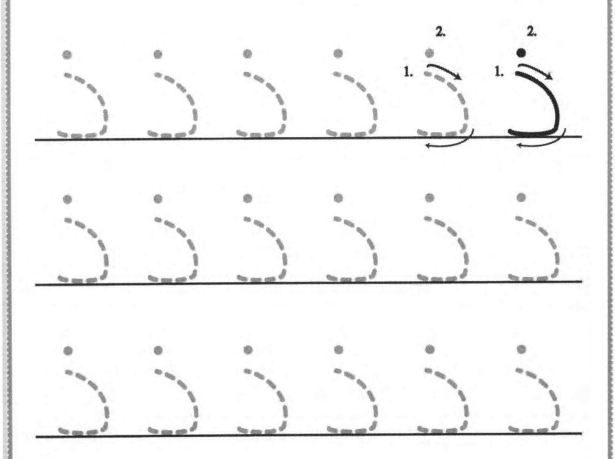

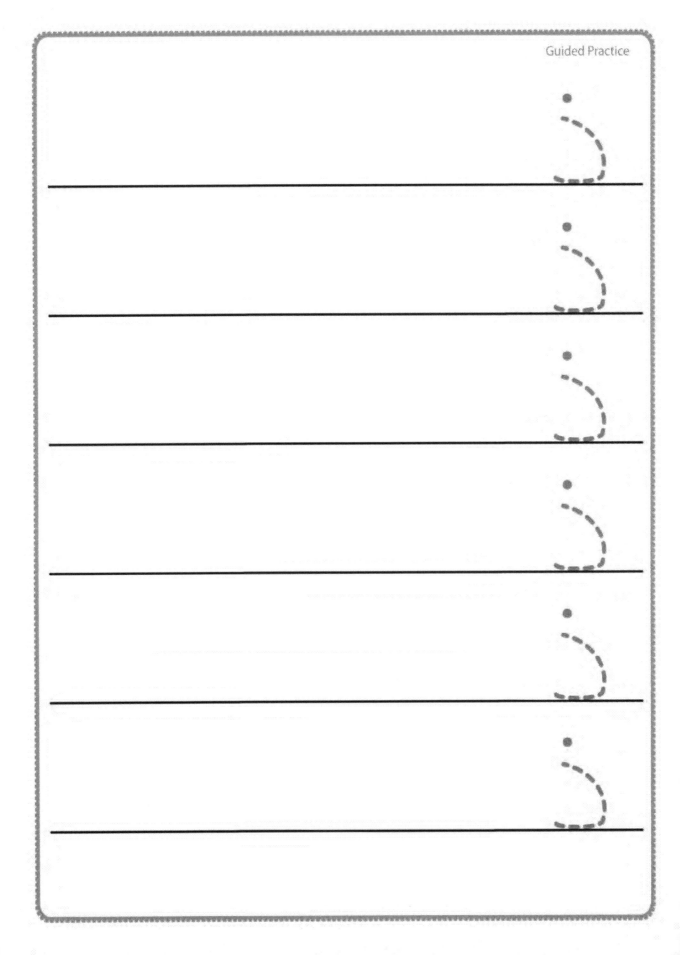

How to write it:
Begin at the top of the letter. Follow the arrow down and around in a curve ending on the left.

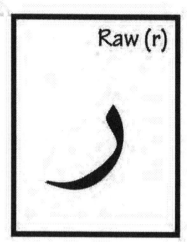

Raw (r)

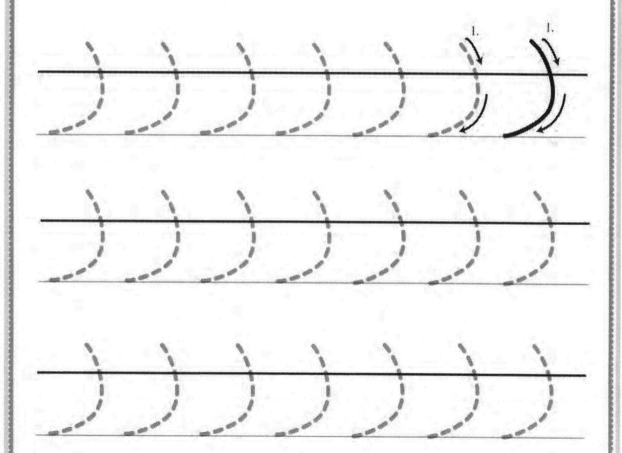

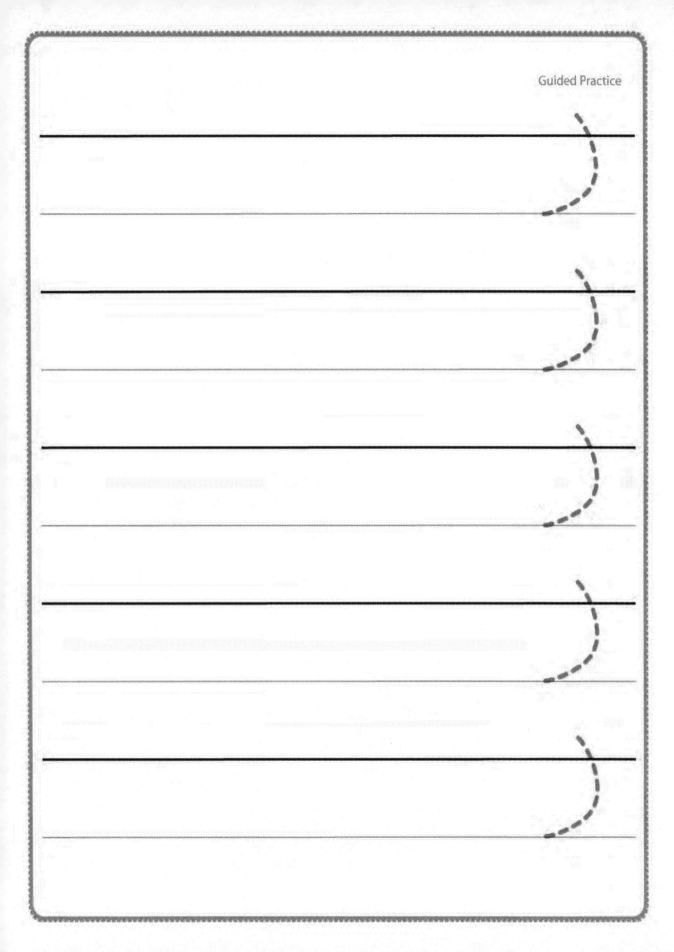

Lesson: 11

How to write it:
Begin at the top of the letter. Follow the arrow down and around in a curve ending on the left.

Zaay (z)

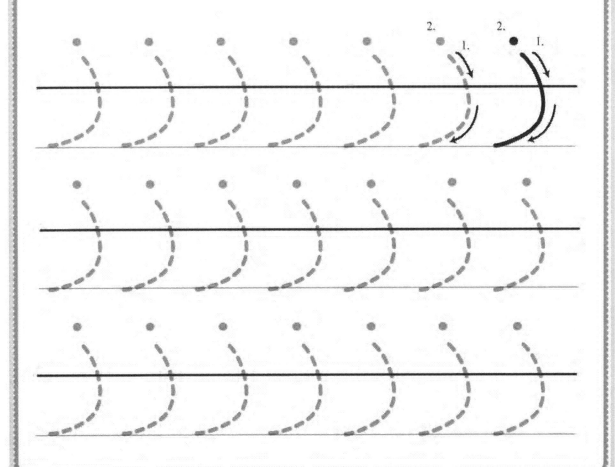

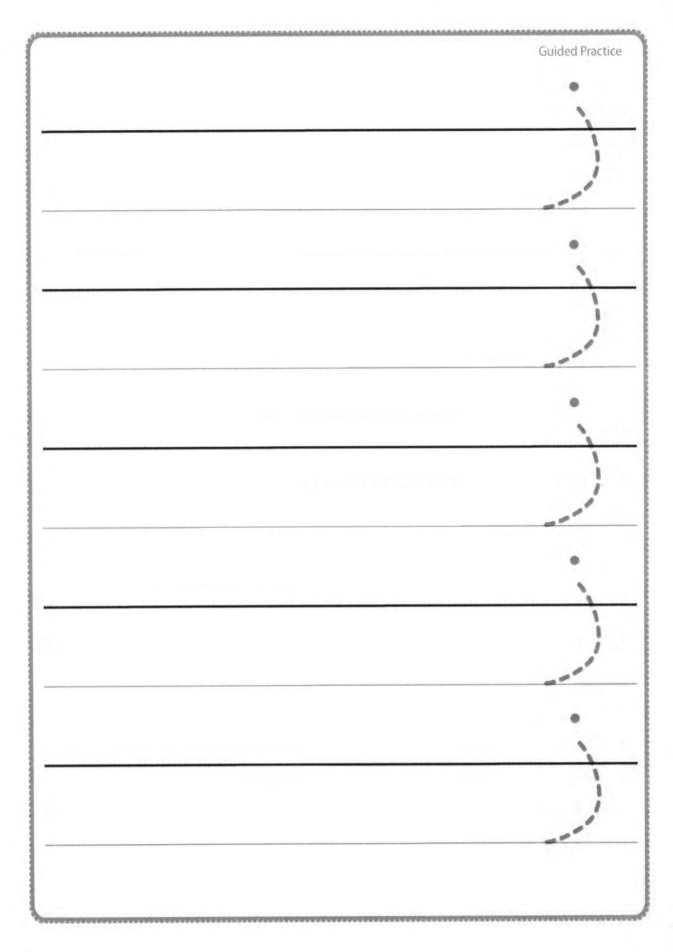

How to write it:

The head of this letter rests on the line. Begin from the right with a u-shaped curve, repeat this movement and then follow the arrow as it swoops under the line in a wider curve.

Seen (s)

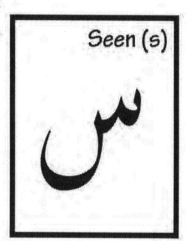

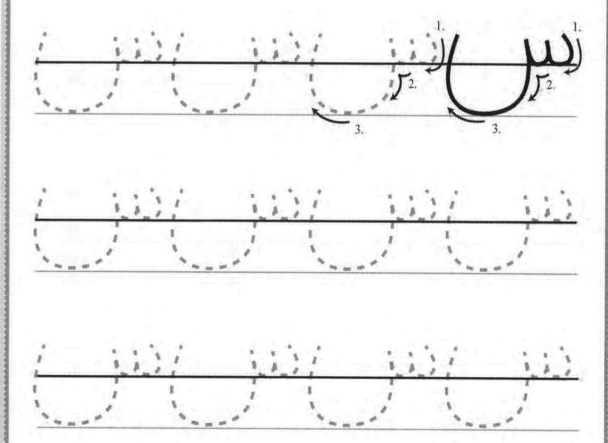

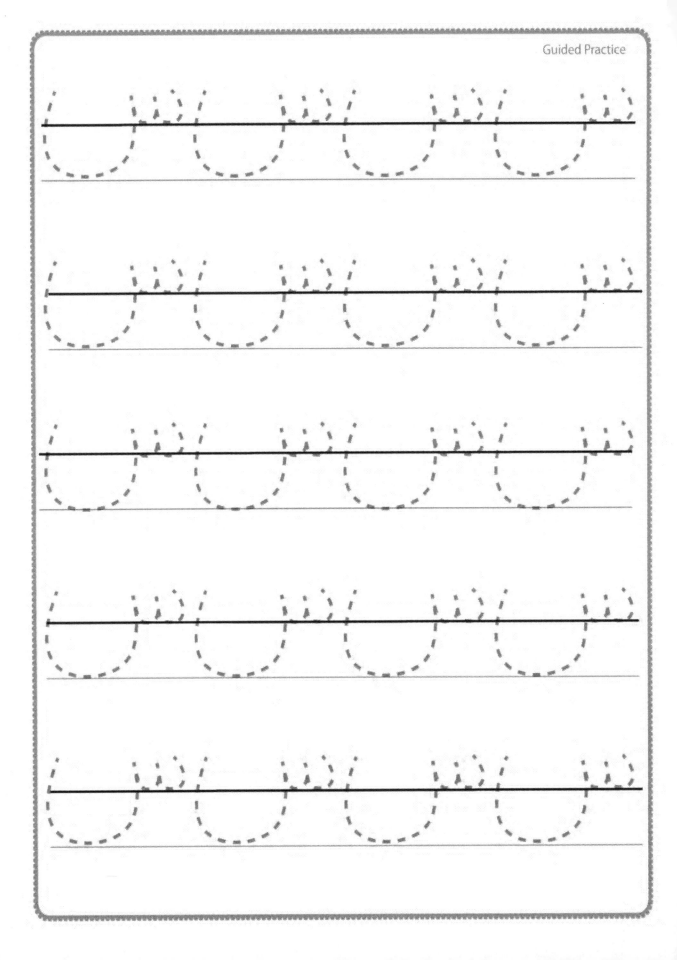

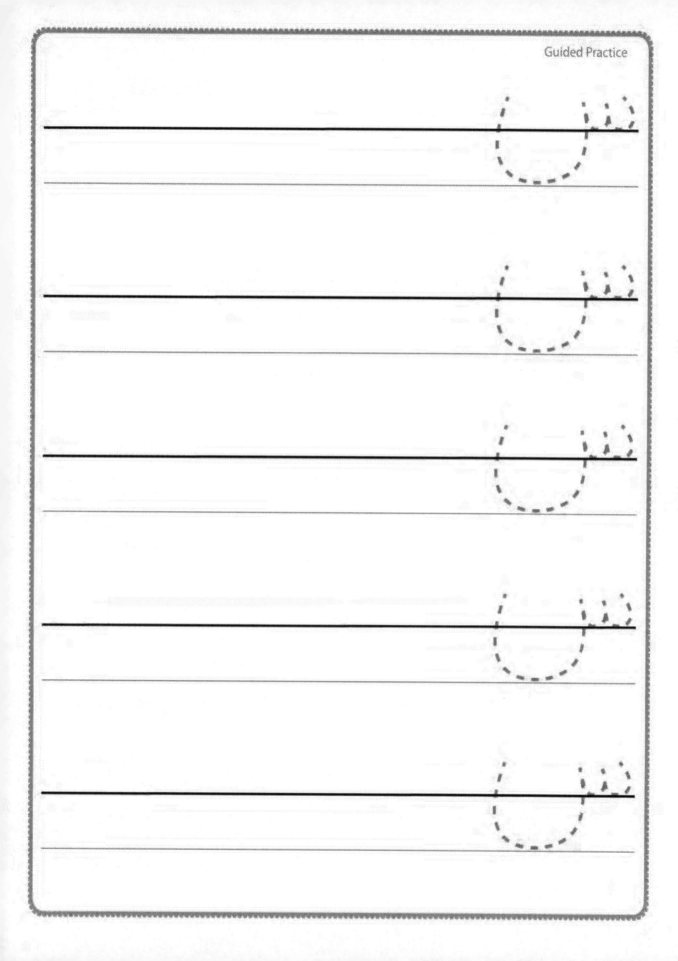

Lesson: 13

How to write it:
The head of this letter rests on the line. Begin from the right with a u-shaped curve, repeat this movement and then follow the arrow as it swoops under the line in a wider curve. Place three dots above the letter.

Sheen (s)

ش

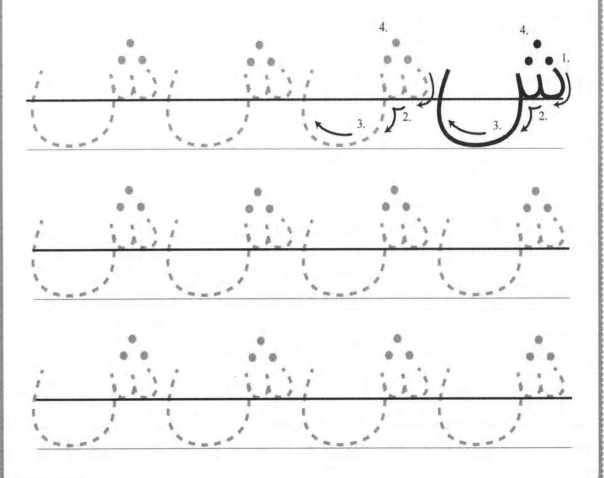

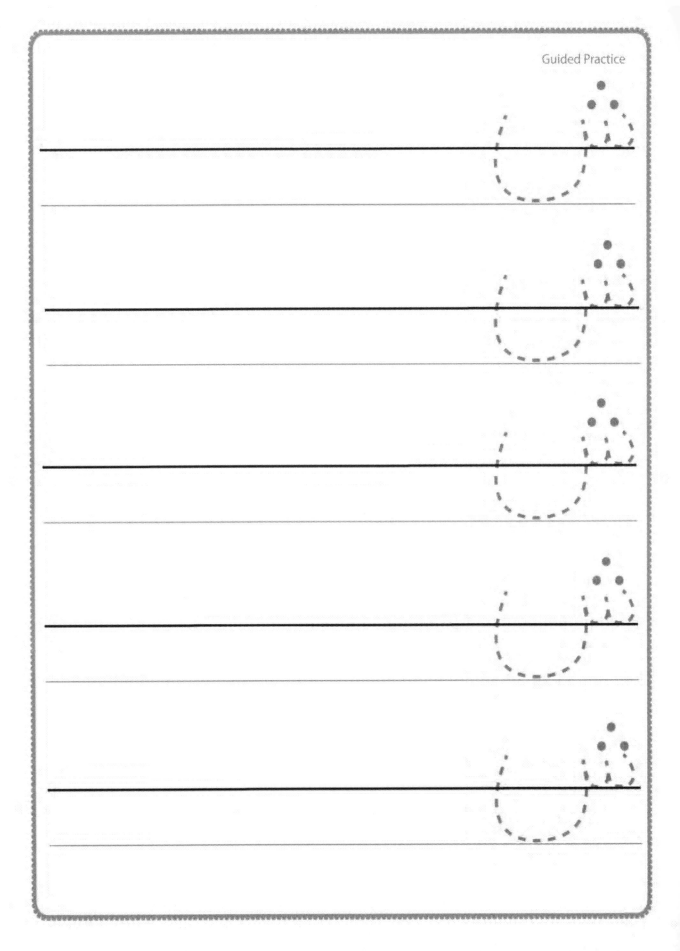

How to write it:

The head of this letter rests on the line. Begin by drawing a loop, and then follow the arrow as it swoops under the line in a wide curve.

Sawd (s)

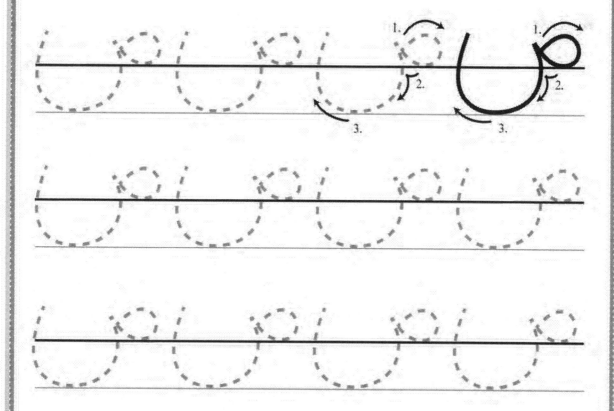

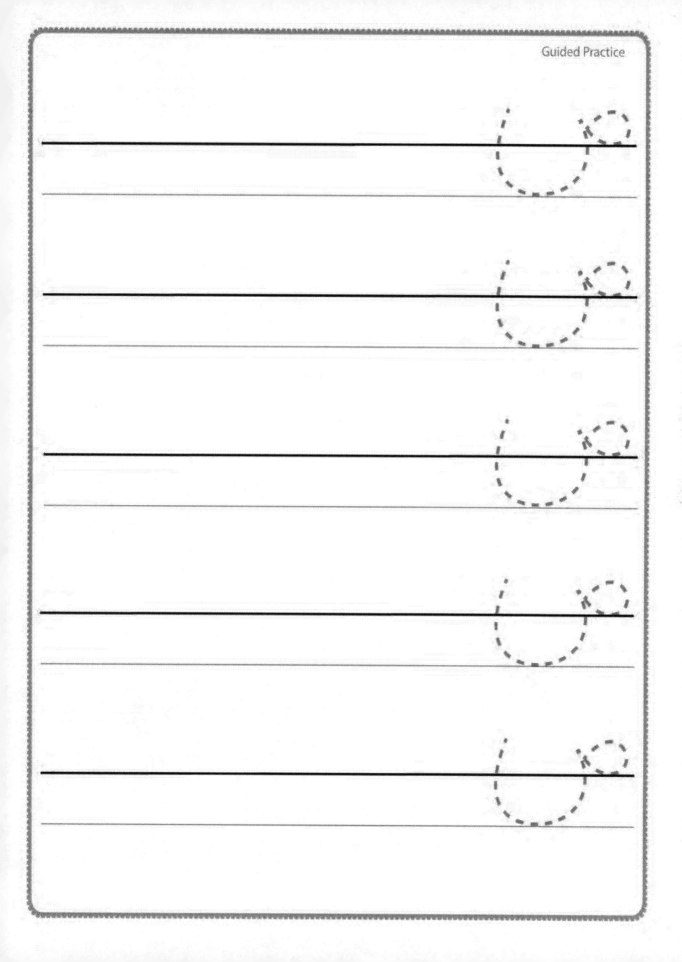

How to write it:

The head of this letter rests on the line. Begin by drawing a loop, and then follow the arrow as it swoops under the line in a wide curve. Place a dot above the letter.

Dawd (d)

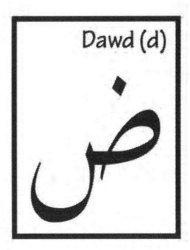

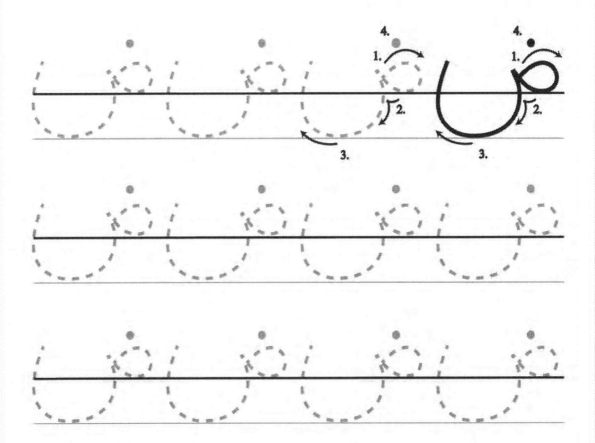

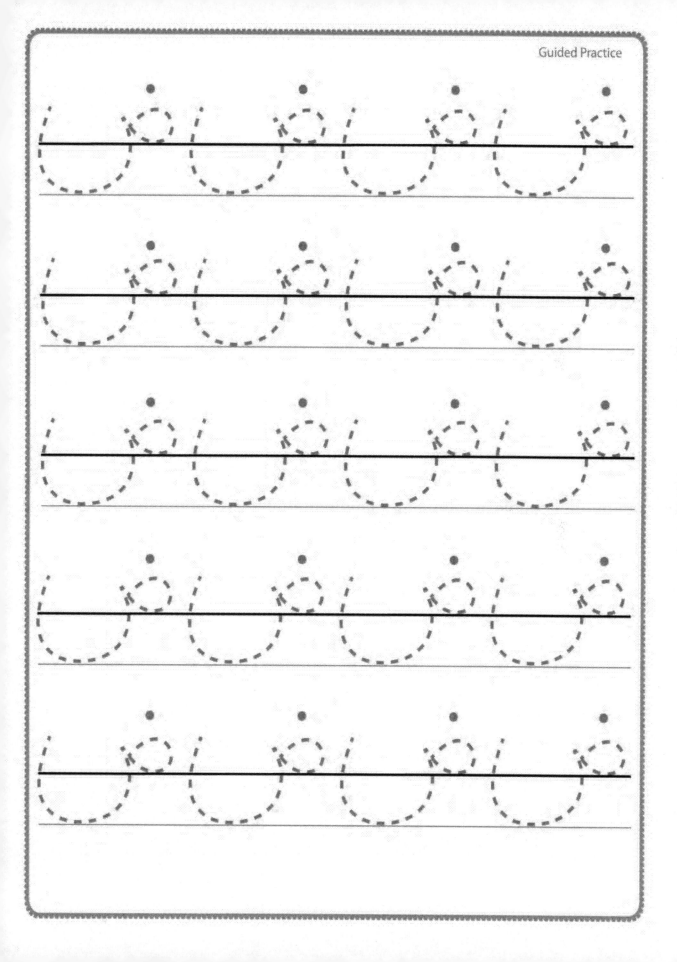

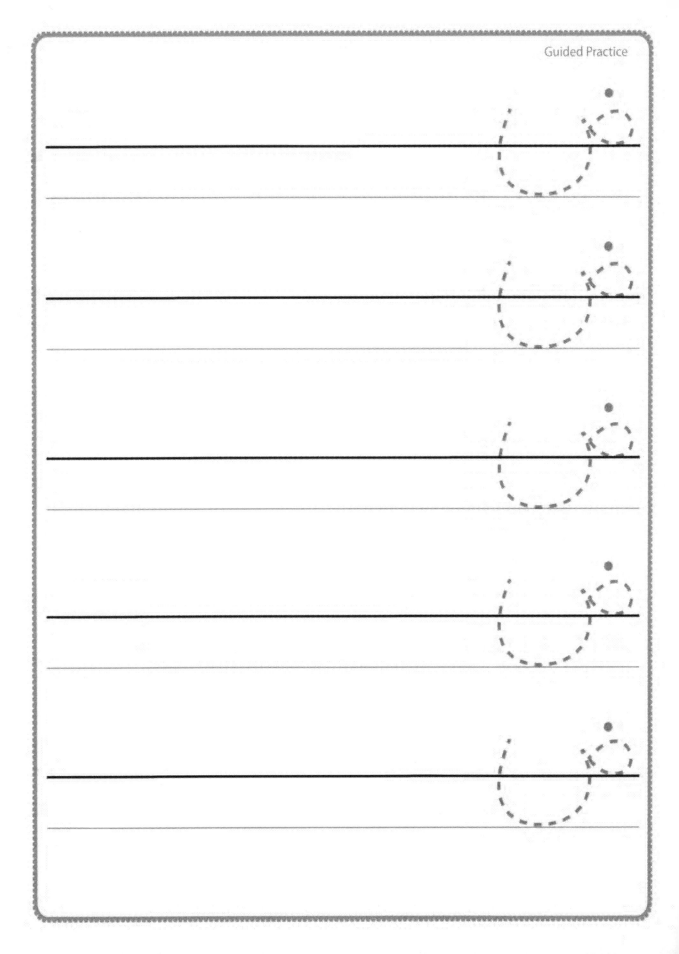

Lesson: 16

How to write it:
Begin by drawing a complete loop, and then draw a line straight down to meet the top of the loop.

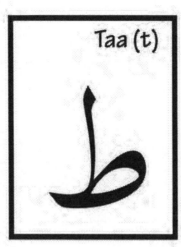

Taa (t)

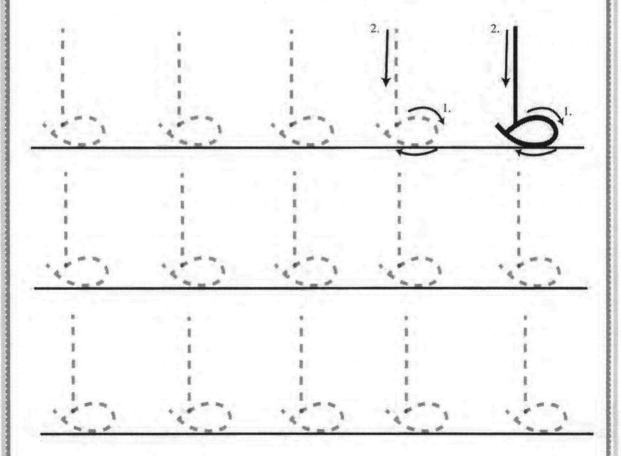

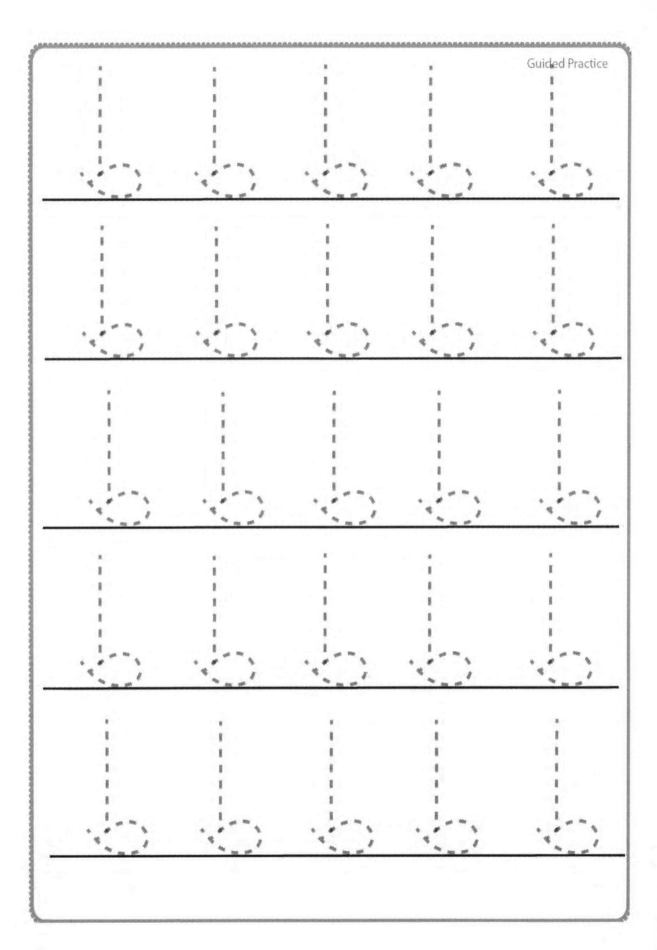

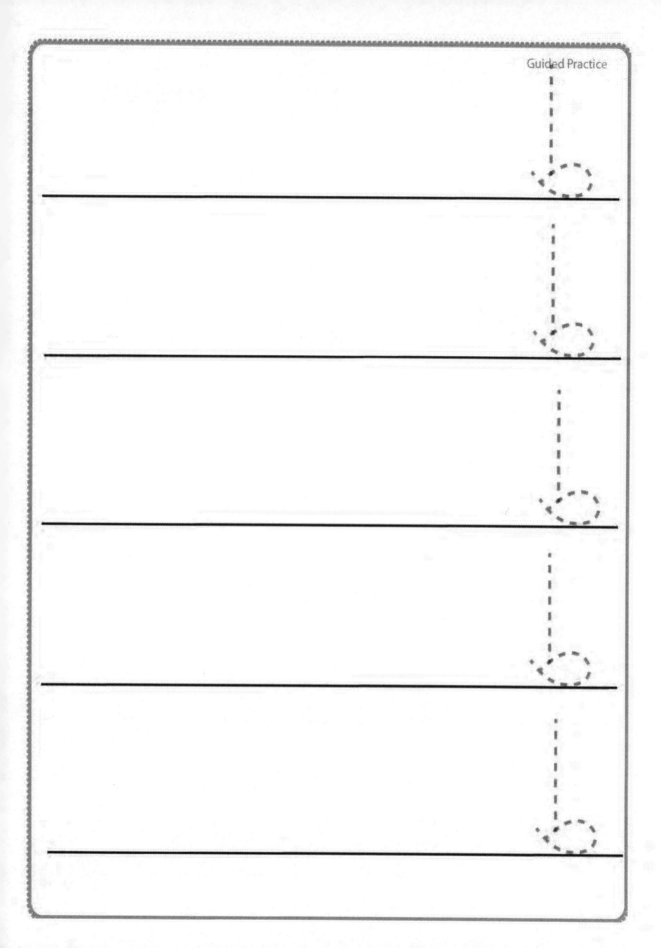

How to write it:
Begin by drawing a complete loop, and then draw a line straight down to meet the top of the loop. Place a dot above the loop.

Zaa (z)

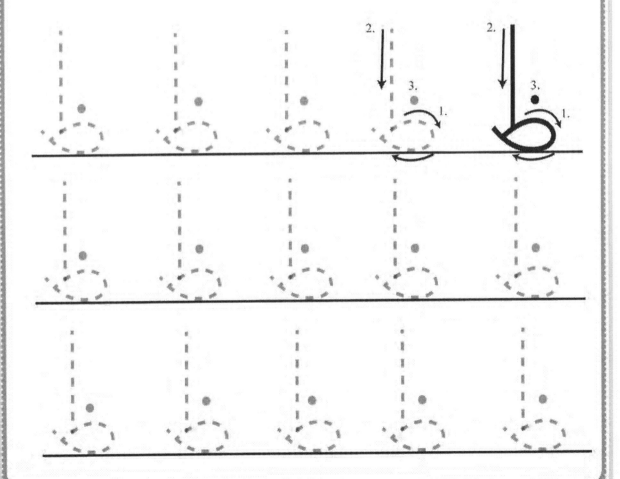

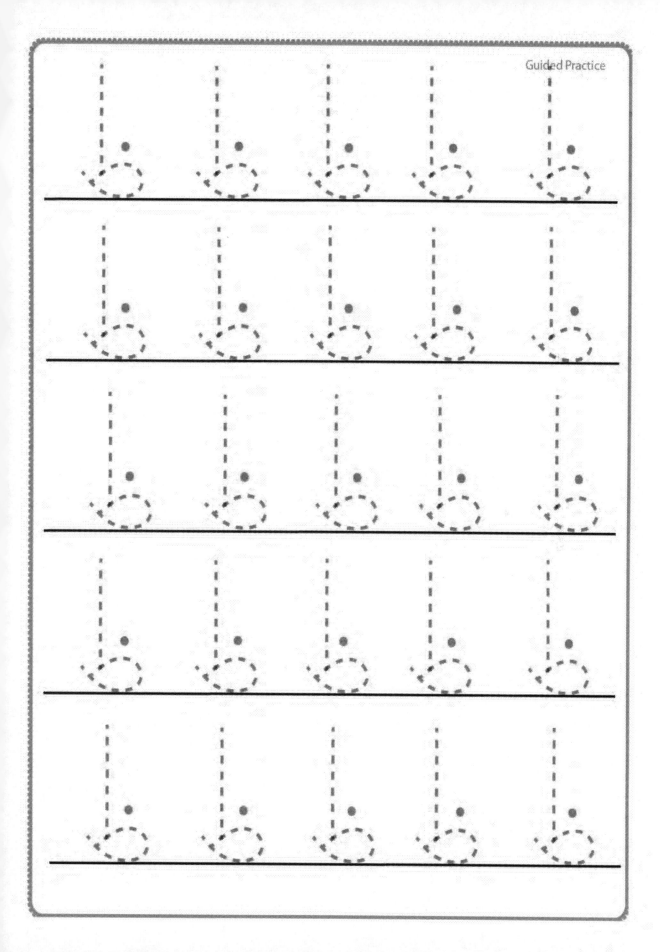

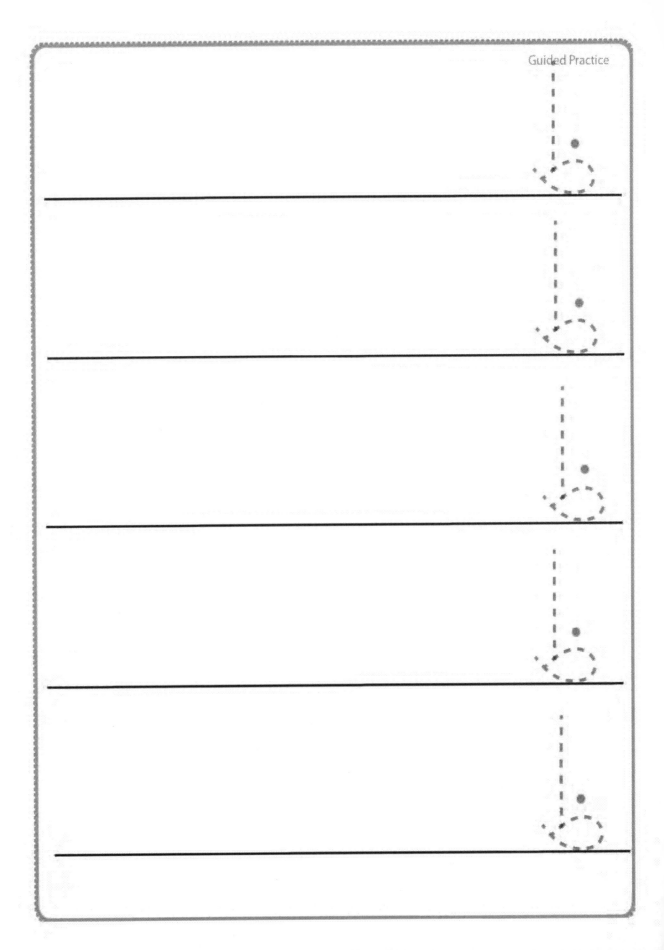

How to write it:

The head of this letter rests on the line. Begin with a curve for the head and follow the arrow around in a larger curve just under it.

'Ayn ('a)

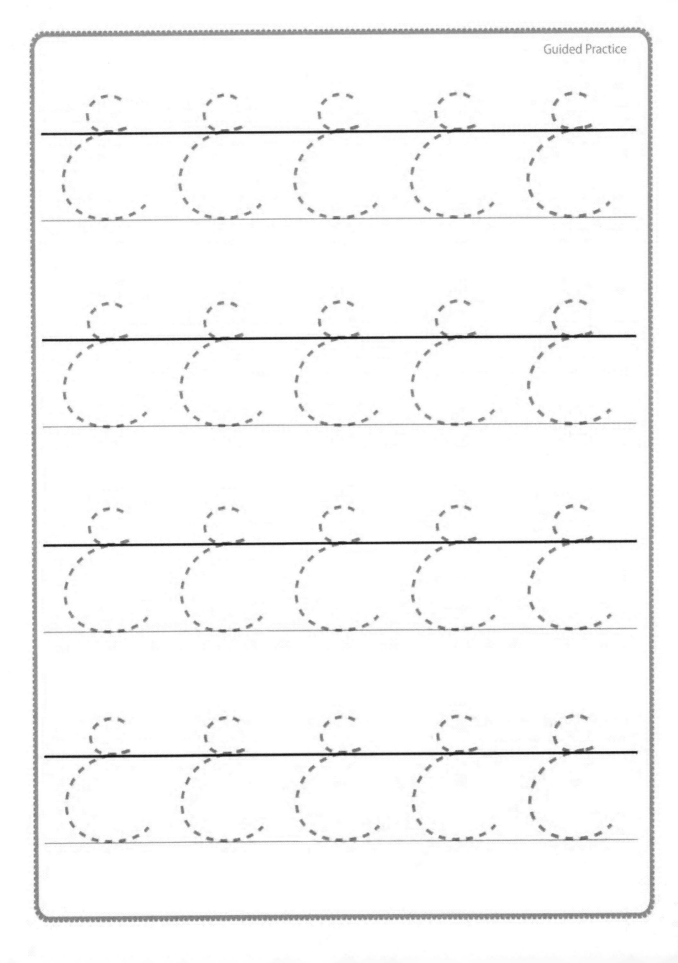

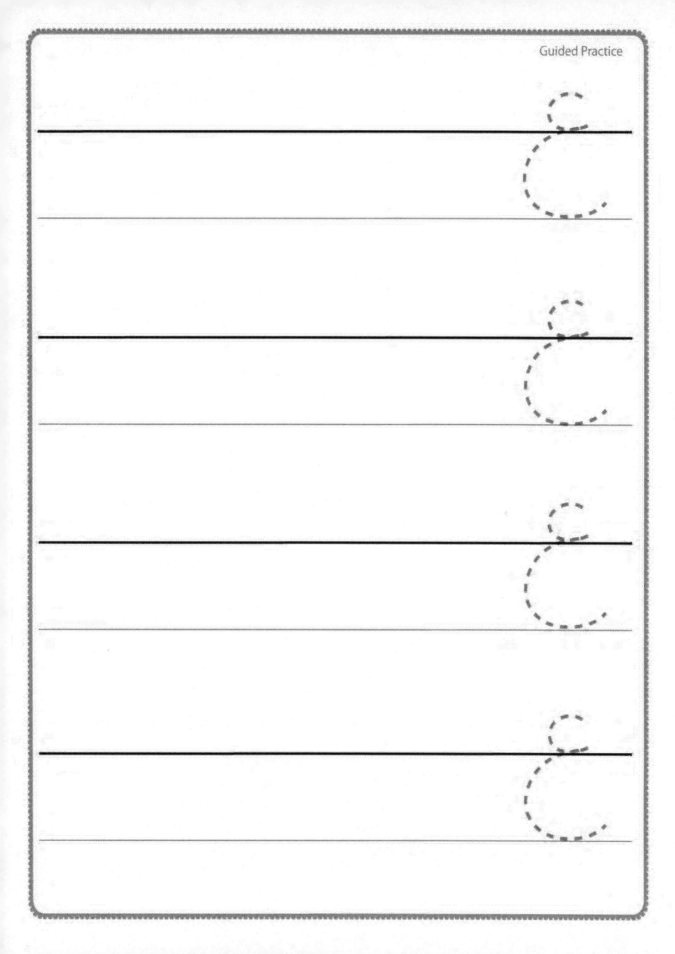

How to write it:
The head of this letter rests on the line. Begin with a curve for the head and follow the arrow around in a larger curve just under it. Draw a dot above the letter.

Ghayn (g)

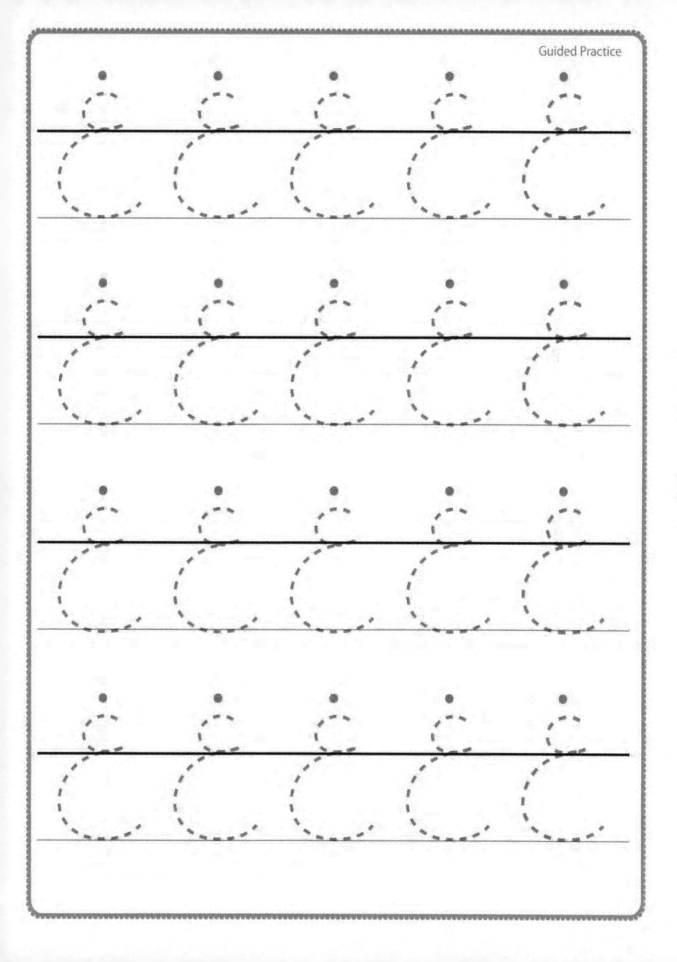

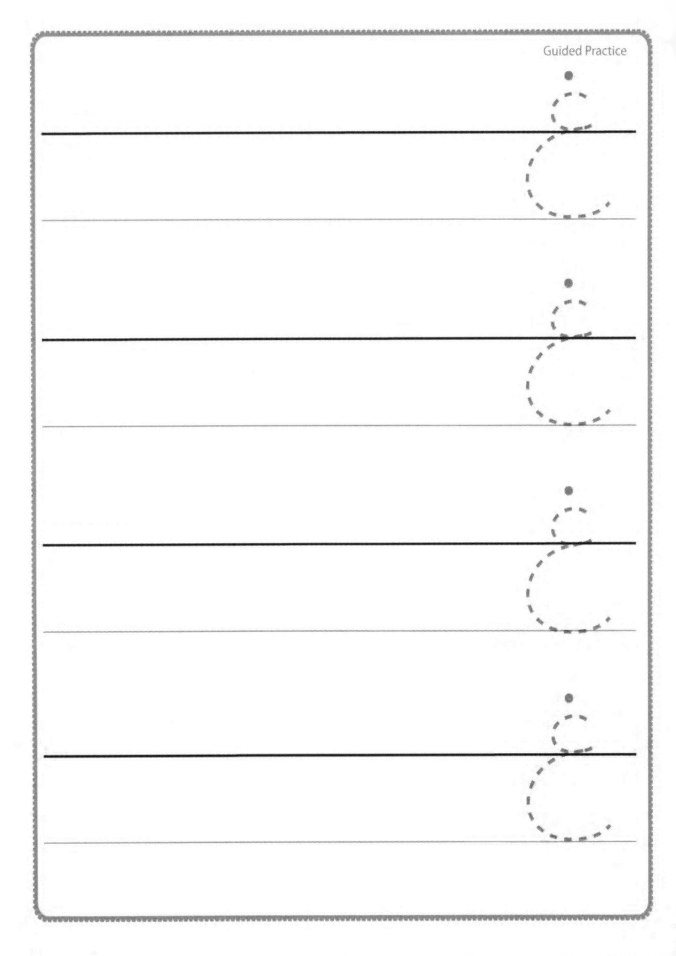

How to write it:
Start by drawing a circle. Extend the tail end along the line towards the left and back up. Draw a dot above the letter.

Faa (f)

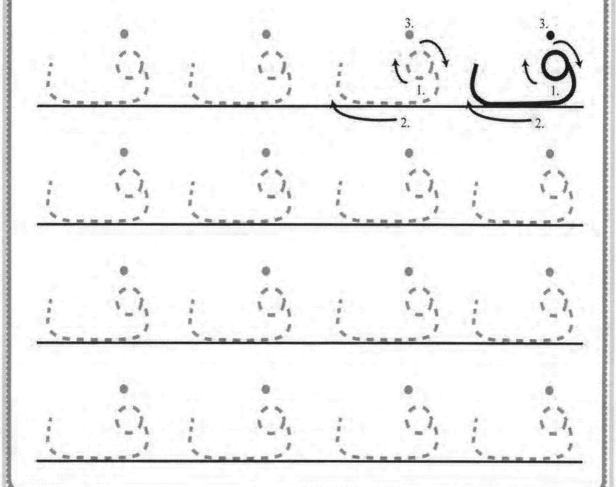

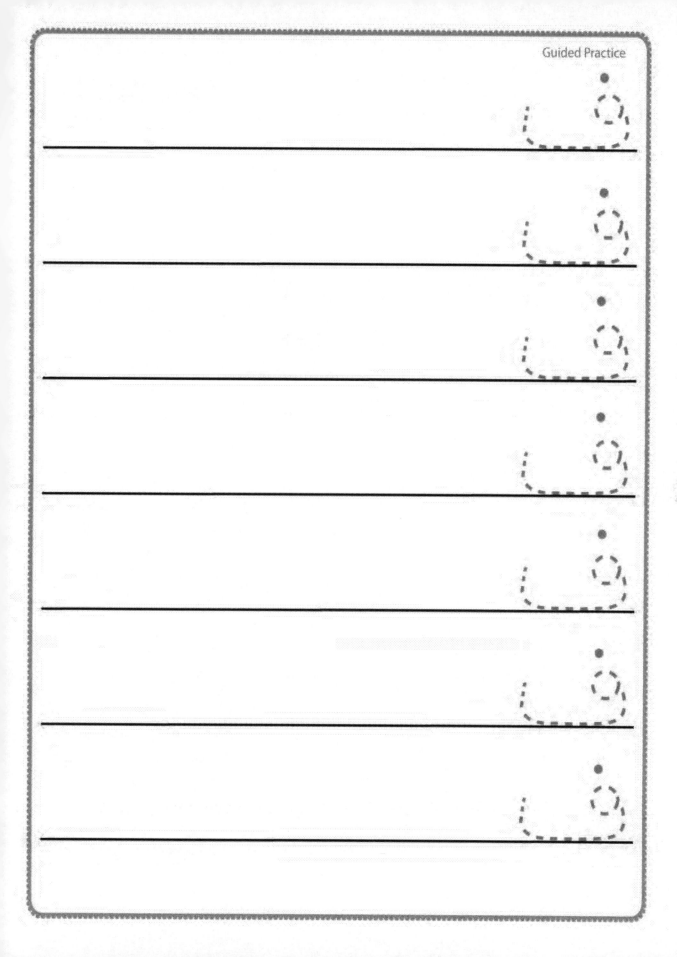

How to write it:
Start by drawing a circle. Extend the tail end in a wider circle under the line and back up. Draw two dots above the letter.

Qaaf (q)

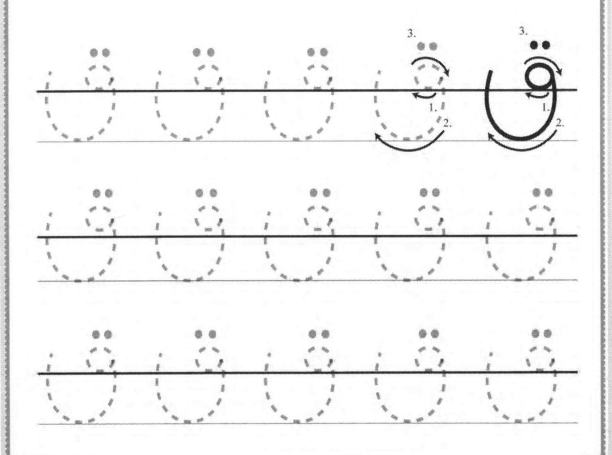

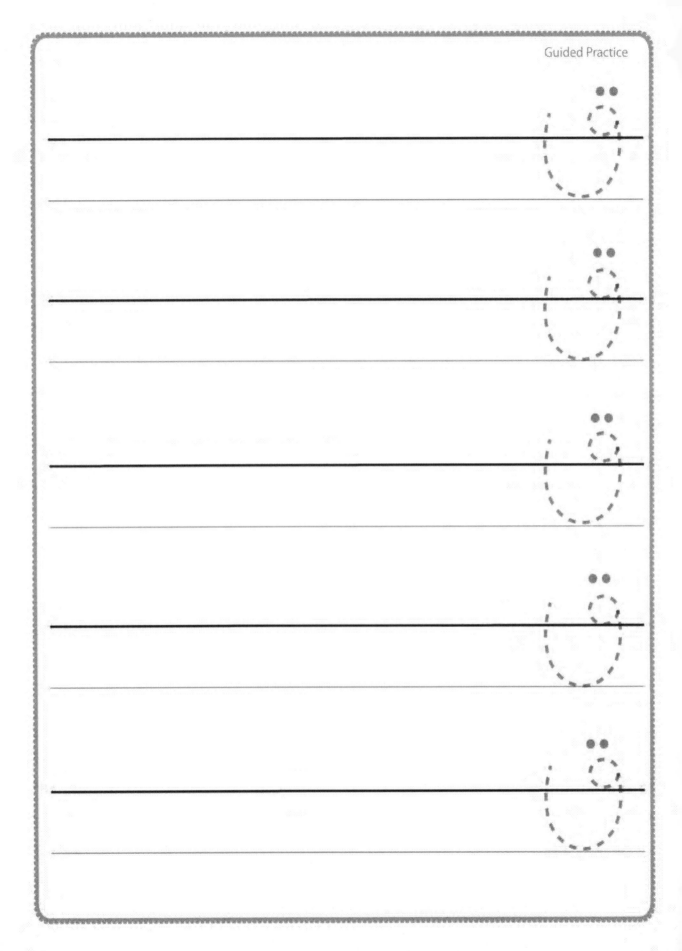

How to write it:
Begin by drawing a straight line down, and then follow the arrows across the bottom in a straight line. Finish by drawing an s-shaped swirl inside the letter.

Kaaf (k)

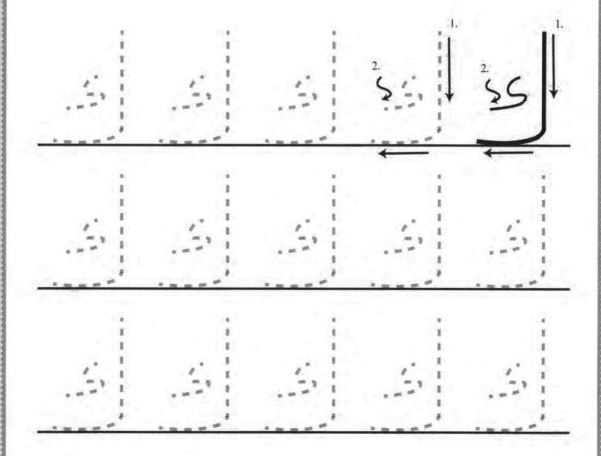

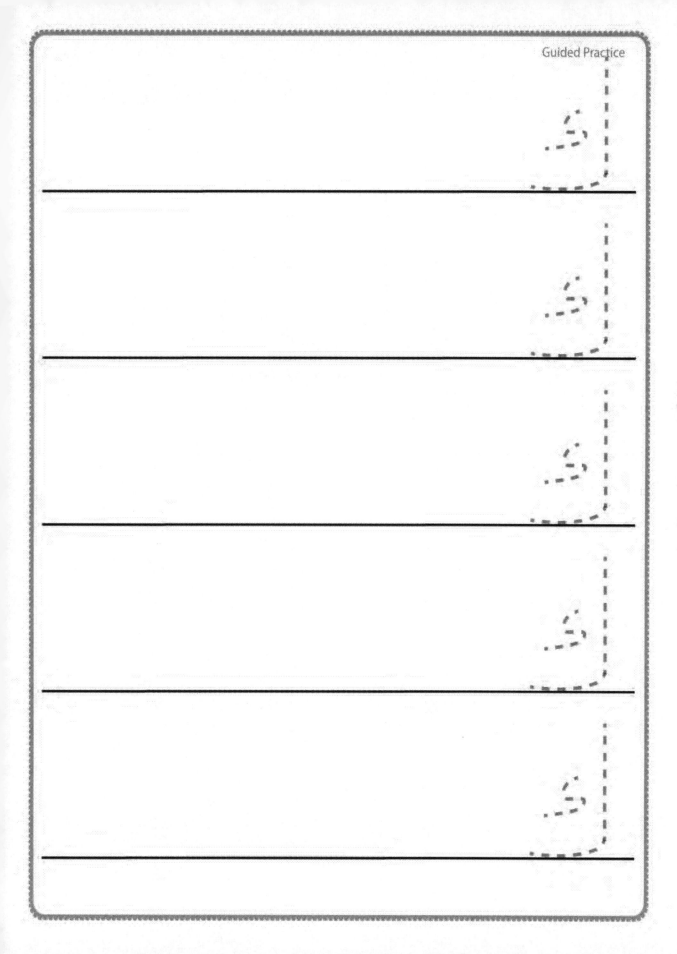

How to write it:
Start by drawing a line straight down.
Extend the tail around in a loop.

Laam (l)

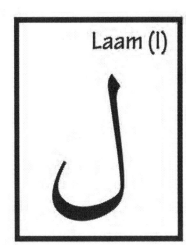

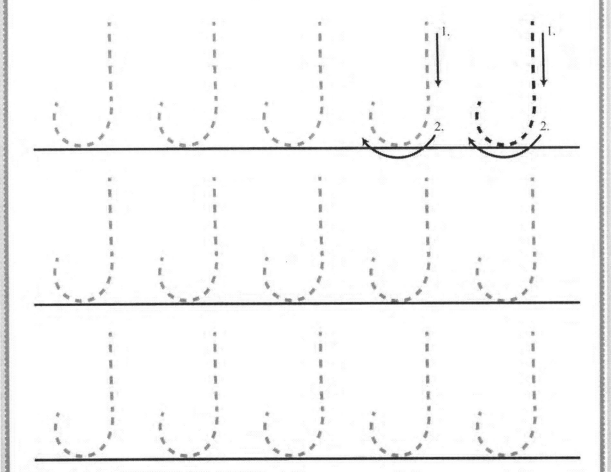

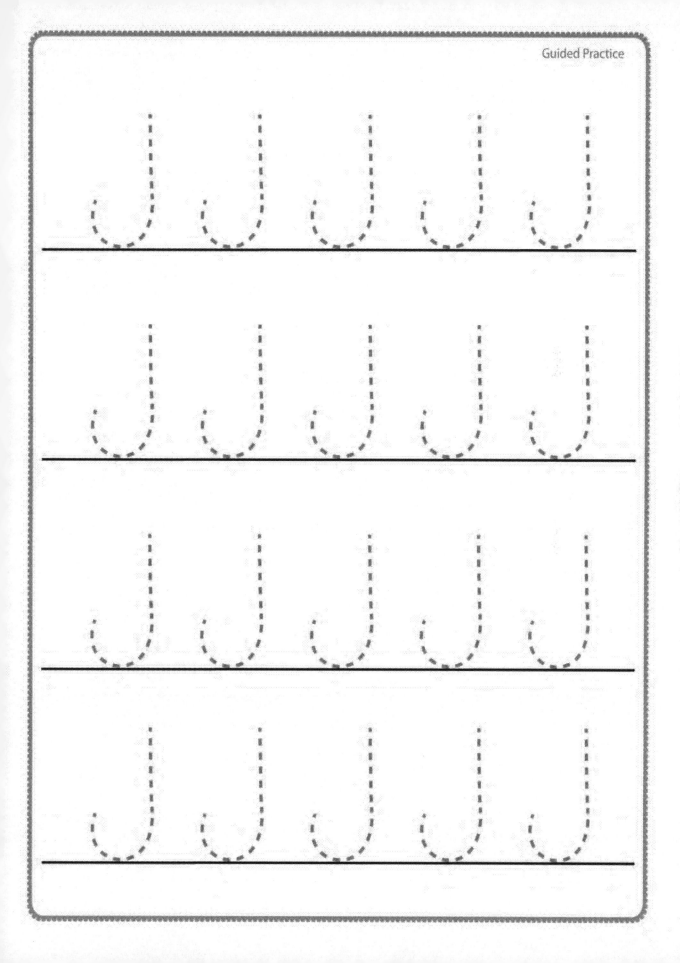

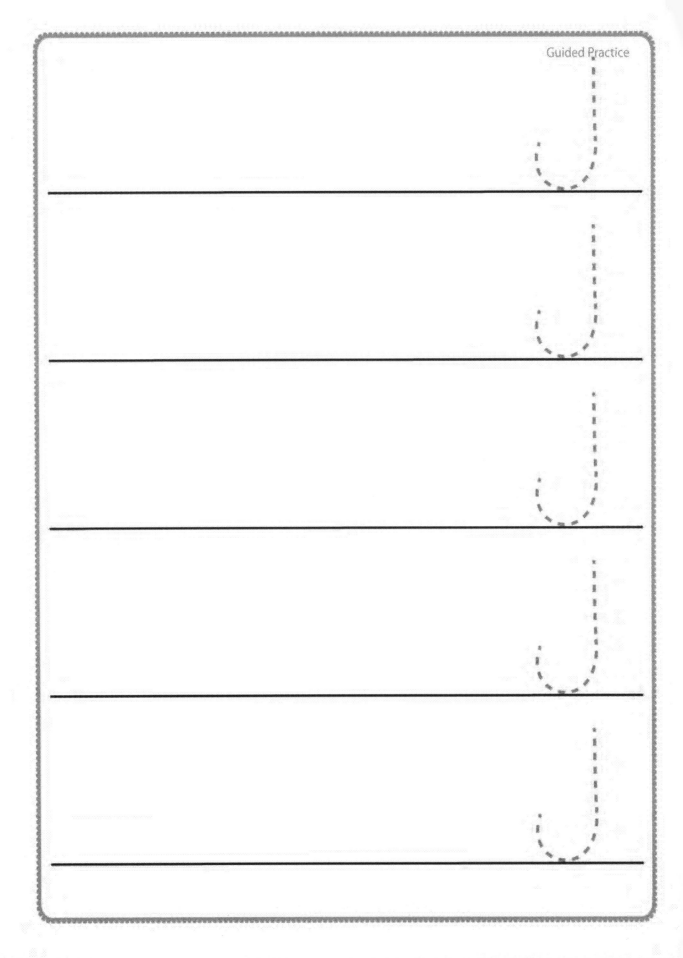

How to write it:
Start by drawing a circle. Extend the taili
end straight down below the line.

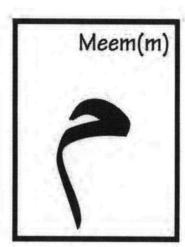

Meem(m)

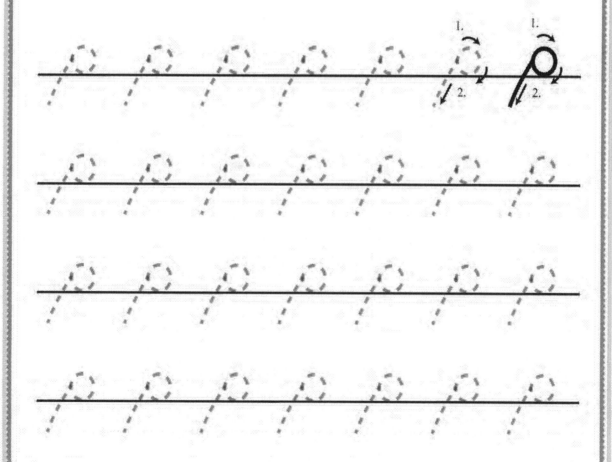

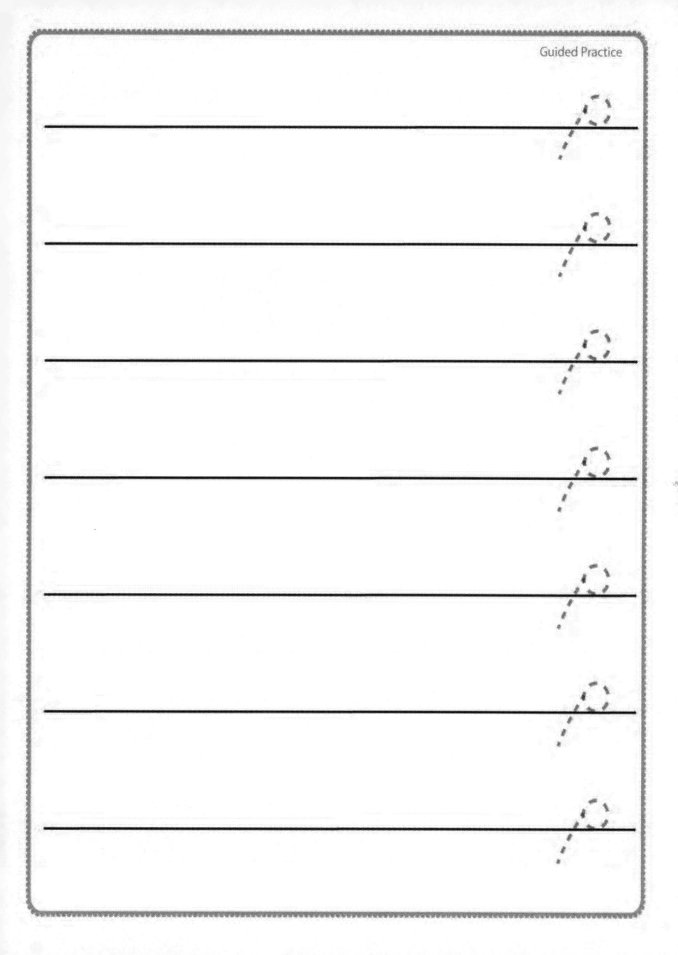

Lesson: 25

How to write it:
Follow the arrows in a clockwise half circle. Draw one dot above the letter.

Noon(n)

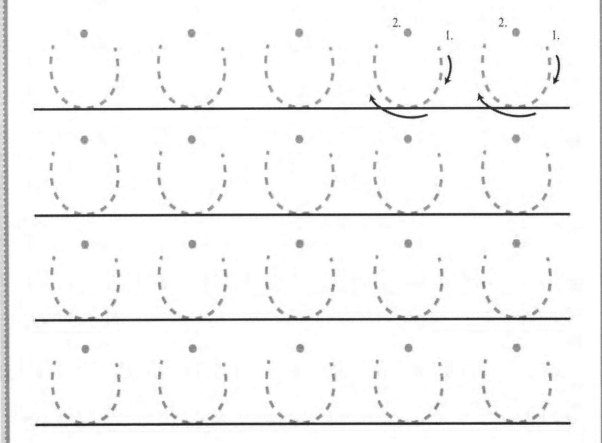

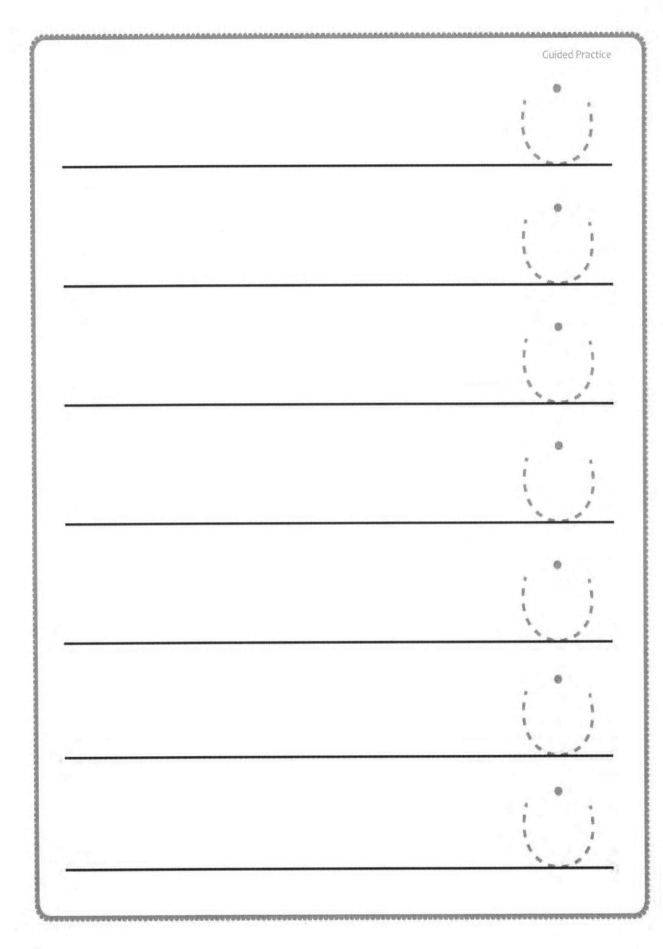

How to write it:
Start at the top of the letter. This letter begins with a swirl and then loops before extending out in a short tail.

haa(h)

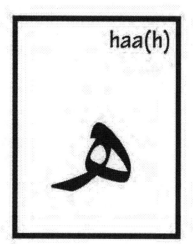

How its done!

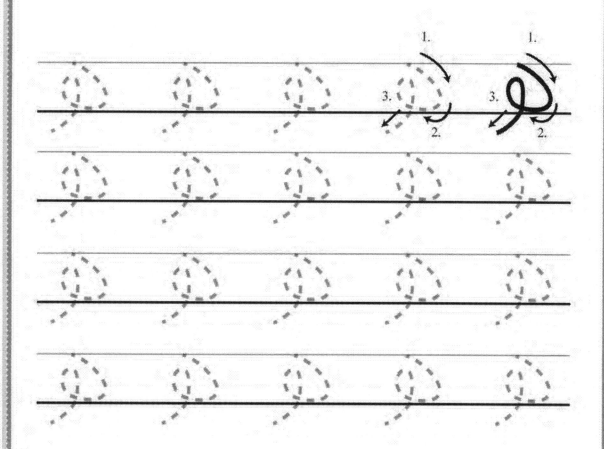

How to write it:
Start by drawing a cirlce. Extend the tail end.

Waaw (w)

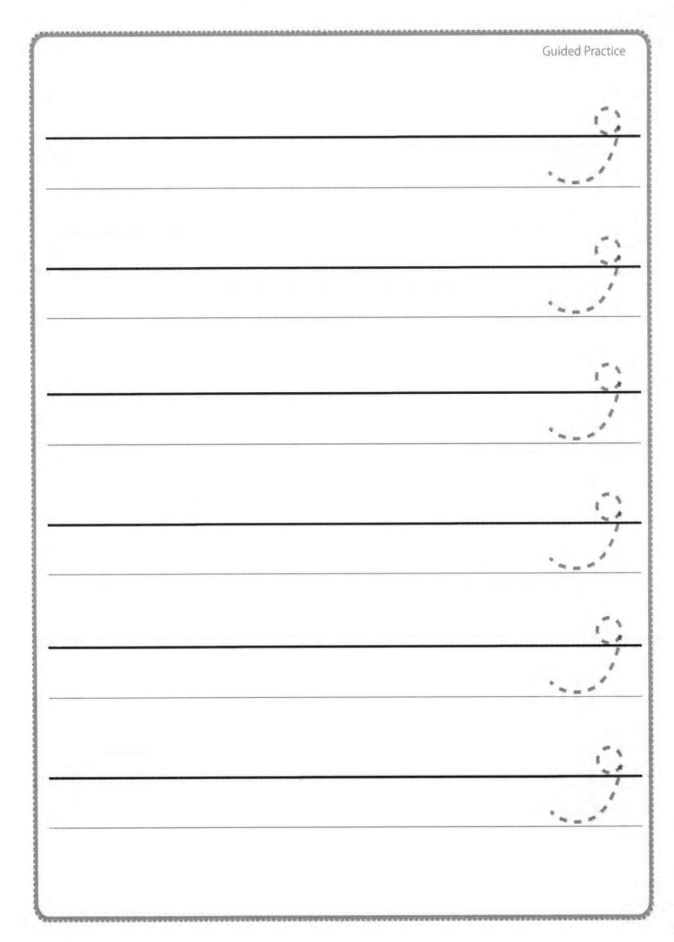

Lesson: 28

How to write it:

The head of this letter rests on the line. Draw the curve of the head and follow the arrows as they swirl around in an s-shaped curve before coming back up. Draw two dots under the letter.

Yaa (y)

ى

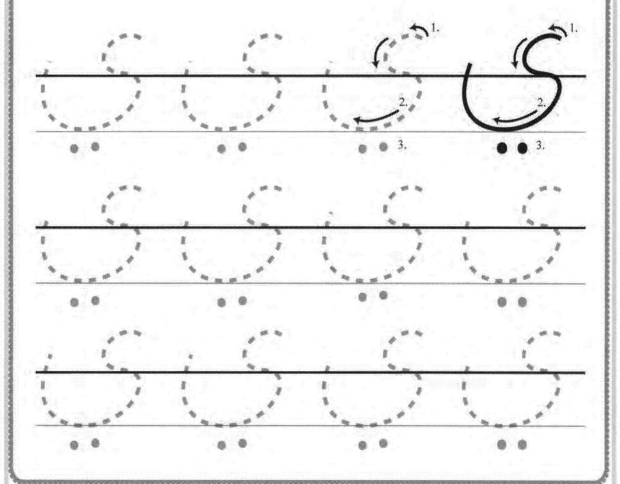

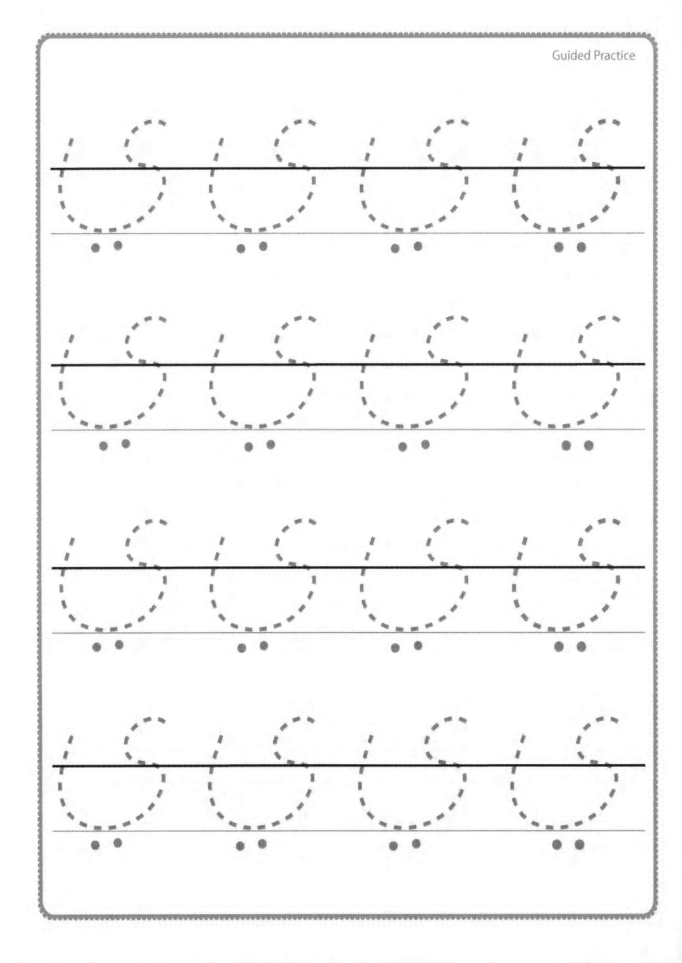

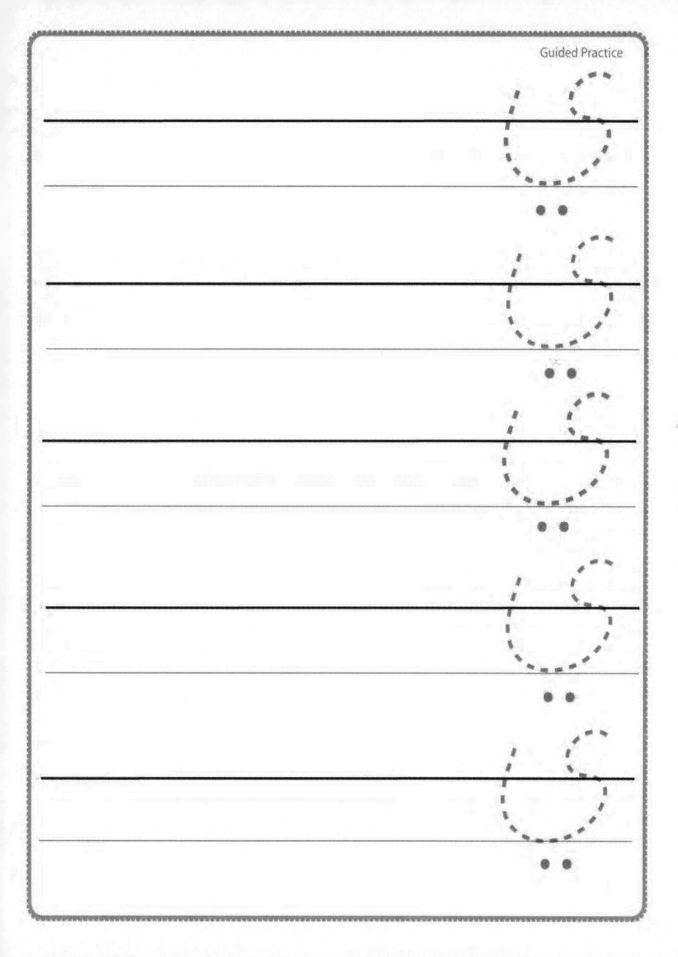

Section 6 : Answer Sheets

In This Section
- ▶ Answer Sheets
- ▶ Answers to the Section Quizzes

 Let's check our answers!

Answer Sheet.

Uu	Ii	Aa	Ii	Aa	Uu
Uu	Aa	Ii	Uu	Aa	Ii
Aa	Ii	Ii	Aa	Ii	Aa
Ii	Aa	Aa	Ii	Uu	Aa
Uu	Aa	Aa	Uu	Ii	Uu
Ii	Ii	Aa	Uu	Aa	Ii
Uu	Uu	Ii	Uu	Ii	Aa

Answer Sheet.

Bi	Ba	Bi	Ba	Bi	Bu
Bi	Bi	Bi	Bu	Bu	Bi
Ba	Bi	Bu	Bi	Ba	Bu
Bu	Bu	Ba	Bu	Ba	Ba
Bi	Ba	Bi	Ba	Bi	Ba
Bi	Bi	Bu	Bi	Ba	Bi
Ba	Bu	Bi	Ba	Bu	Ba
Ba	Bu	Ba	Bu	Bi	Bu

Read each row from right to left.

Ti	Ta	Tu	Ti	Tu	Ta
Tu	Ta	Ti	Tu	Ta	Ta
Ta	Ti	Tu	Ti	Ta	Ta
Tu	Ta	Tu	Tu	Ti	Tu
Ta	Ti	Tu	Ta	Ti	Ti
Ti	Ti	Ti	Ta	Tu	Ta
Tu	Ti	Ti	Tu	Ti	Tu
Tu	Ti	Ta	Tu	Ti	Ta

Answer Sheet.

Tha	Thi	Thu	Tha	Thi	Tha
Tha	Thi	Tha	Thu	Thi	Thu
Thi	Tha	Thu	Thi	Thi	Thu
Tha	Thi	Thu	Tha	Thi	Thu
Thu	Thi	Tha	Thu	Tha	Thi
Thi	Thu	Thu	Thi	Thi	Tha
Tha	Thi	Thu	Tha	Thi	Tha
Thi	Thu	Tha	Thu	Thi	Tha

Read each row from right to left.

Ji	Ja	Ji	Ja	Ju	Ja
Ju	Ji	Ji	Ju	Ja	Ji
Ja	Ja	Ju	Ja	Ji	Ju
Ji	Ju	Ji	Ja	Ju	Ja
Ju	Ja	Ji	Ja	Ji	Ju
Ju	Ji	Ju	Ji	Ji	Ju
Ji	Ja	Ji	Ja	Ju	Ja

Read each row from right to left.

Ha	Hi	Ha	Hi	Hu	Ha
Hi	Hu	Ha	Hi	Ha	Hi
Ha	Hu	Hu	Ha	Hi	Hu
Ha	Hu	Hi	Hu	Hi	Ha
Ha	Ha	Hu	Hi	Hu	Hi
Hi	Ha	Hi	Hu	Hi	Ha
Ha	Ha	Hi	Ha	Ha	Hu

Read each row from right to left.

Kha	Khi	Khu	Khu	Kha	Khu
Khu	Kha	Kha	Khu	Kha	Khi
Kha	Khi	Khi	Kha	Khu	Khu
Khu	Khi	Khu	Khi	Khi	Kha
Kha	Kha	Khi	Khu	Khi	Khi
Khi	Kha	Kha	Khi	Khu	Kha
Khu	Khu	Kha	Khi	Kha	Khu

Read each row from right to left.

Da	Du	Da	Da	Di
Di	Da	Di	Du	Di
Du	Du	Da	Di	Da
Di	Di	Du	Di	Da
Di	Da	Du	Da	Du
Da	Di	Da	Du	Di
Di	Da	Du	Di	Da
Da	Du	Du	Da	Du

Read each row from right to left.

Dha	Dhi	Dha	Dhu	Dha
Dha	Dhi	Dhi	Dha	Dhi
Dhu	Dha	Dhu	Dhi	Dhu
Dha	Dhi	Dha	Dhu	Dha
Dha	Dhu	Dhi	Dhu	Dhi
Dhi	Dhi	Dhu	Dhi	Dhu
Dhu	Dhu	Dhi	Dha	Dhi
Dhu	Dha	Dha	Dhu	Dha

Read each row from right to left.

Ra	Ru	Ra	Ri	Ri
Ri	Ra	Ri	Ra	Ru
Ra	Ri	Ru	Ri	Ra
Ru	Ra	Ra	Ri	Ru
Ri	Ri	Ru	Ra	Ri
Ra	Ri	Ri	Ru	Ra
Ri	Ri	Ra	Ri	Ru
Ru	Ra	Ru	Ru	Ra

Read each row from right to left.

Zu	Za	Zi	Za	Zu	Za	Zi
Zi	Zu	Za	Zi	Za	Zu	Zu
Zu	Zi	Zi	Zu	Za	Zi	Za
Zi	Zu	Zu	Zu	Za	Za	Zi
Zu	Zi	Zi	Za	Zu	Za	Zu
Zu	Za	Zu	Za	Zi	Zu	Zi
Za	Zu	Zi	Za	Za	Zi	Za
Zi	Za	Zi	Za	Zi	Zi	Za

Read each row from right to left.

Sa	Si	Sa	Su	Su	Si
Si	Sa	Si	Sa	Sa	Su
Si	Sa	Si	Su	Si	Sa
Si	Sa	Su	Si	Sa	Su
Sa	Sa	Si	Sa	Su	Si
Su	Si	Sa	Si	Si	Su
Sa	Su	Si	Sa	Su	Sa

Read each row from right to left.

Sha	Sha	Shu	Sha	Shu
Sha	Shi	Sha	Sha	Shi
Shi	Sha	Shu	Shi	Sha
Sha	Shi	Shi	Sha	Shu
Shi	Shu	Shi	Shu	Shi
Shu	Shi	Sha	Shu	Sha
Shi	Shi	Shu	Sha	Shi

Read each row from right to left.

Su	Sa	Su	Si	Sa
Sa	Si	Sa	Su	Si
Si	Sa	Si	Sa	Su
Sa	Su	Si	Su	Si
Si	Sa	Sa	Su	Sa
Si	Si	Su	Si	Su
Si	Si	Sa	Su	Si
Sa	Si	Si	Su	Sa

Read each row from right to left.

Di	Di	Du	Da	Da
Da	Di	Da	Di	Du
Da	Di	Du	Di	Da
Di	Du	Da	Da	Du
Di	Di	Du	Di	Da
Da	Da	Di	Du	Da
Di	Du	Da	Di	Du
Di	Du	Di	Du	Da

Read each row from right to left.

Ti	Ti	Ti	Tu	Ti	Ta
Ta	Tu	Ti	Ta	Tu	Ti
Ta	Ta	Ta	Tu	Ta	Tu
Ta	Tu	Ta	Ti	Ti	Ta
Tu	Ta	Tu	Ti	Tu	Ti
Ti	Ti	Ta	Tu	Ti	Ta
Tu	Ta	Tu	Ti	Tu	Ti

Read each row from right to left.

Zi	Zu	Zi	Za	Zu	Za
Zu	Zi	Zu	Zi	Za	Zu
Za	Za	Zi	Za	Za	Zi
Zi	Zi	Za	Za	Zu	Za
Za	Zi	Za	Zi	Za	Zi
Zi	Zi	Zu	Za	Zi	Zu

Read each row from right to left.

Ii	Aa	Aa	Ii	Uu	Aa
Uu	Ii	Aa	Ii	Aa	Uu
Uu	Aa	Ii	Uu	Aa	Ii
Aa	Ii	Ii	Aa	Ii	Aa
Ii	Ii	Aa	Uu	Aa	Ie
Uu	Uu	Ii	Uu	Ii	Aa

Read each row from right to left.

Gha	Ghi	Ghi	Gha	Ghi	Gha	Ghu
Ghi	Gha	Gha	Ghi	Ghu	Ghi	Gha
Ghu	Ghi	Ghi	Ghu	Gha	Gha	Ghi
Gha	Gha	Ghi	Gha	Ghu	Ghu	Ghi
Ghu	Ghu	Ghu	Ghi	Gha	Ghi	Ghi
Gha	Ghi	Ghi	Gha	Ghu	Gha	Ghi

Read each row from right to left.

Fi	Fa	Fa	Fi	Fu	Fa
Fu	Fi	Fa	Fi	Fa	Fu
Fu	Fa	Fi	Fu	Fa	Fi
Fa	Fi	Fi	Fa	Fi	Fa
Fi	Fi	Fa	Fu	Fa	Fi
Fu	Fu	Fi	Fu	Fi	Fa
Fu	Fa	Fa	Fu	Fi	Fu

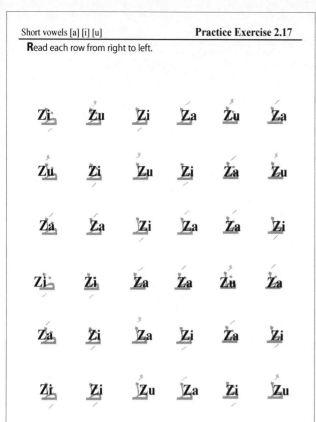

Read each row from right to left.

Qa	Qa	Qi	Qa	Qu	Qi
Qa	Qi	Qu	Qu	Qa	Qi
Qi	Qa	Qu	Qi	Qa	Qu
Qi	Qi	Qa	Qa	Qi	Qa
Qa	Qi	Qi	Qi	Qa	Qu
Qi	Qu	Qu	Qa	Qi	Qu

Read each row from right to left.

Ki	Ki	Ka	Ka	Ka	Ku
Ki	Ku	Ki	Ka	Ku	Ka
Ku	Ku	Ka	Ki	Ki	Ka
Ka	Ka	Ki	Ki	Ka	Ki
Ku	Ki	Ki	Ka	Ki	Ka
Ku	Ki	Ku	Ka	Ka	Ki

Read each row from right to left.

La	Lu	Li	La	La	Li
Lu	La	Li	La	Li	Lu
Li	La	Lu	Li	La	Lu
La	Li	La	Li	Li	La
Li	La	Lu	La	Li	Li
La	Li	Lu	Li	Lu	Lu

Read each row from right to left.

Ma	Mu	Mi	Ma	Ma	Mi
Mu	Ma	Mi	Ma	Mi	Mu
Mi	Ma	Mu	Mi	Ma	Mu
Ma	Mi	Ma	Mi	Mi	Ma
Mi	Mi	Mu	Ma	Mi	Mi
Ma	Mi	Mu	Mi	Mu	Mu

Read each row from right to left.

Nu	Na	Ni	Na	Ni	Na
Na	Nu	Ni	Na	Nu	Ni
Na	Ni	Nu	Ni	Nu	Na
Ni	Na	Na	Ni	Na	Ni
Na	Ni	Nu	Na	Ni	Ni
Ni	Na	Nu	Ni	Nu	Nu

ha	ha	hi	hu	ha
hi	hi	hu	ha	hi
hi	hi	hu	hu	ha
hu	hu	hi	ha	hi
hu	hi	ha	hi	hu
hu	hi	hi	ha	hi
hu	ha	ha	hu	hi

Read each row from right to left.

Wi	Wi	Wa	Wu	Wa	Wi
Wi	Wa	Wa	Wi	Wu	Wa
Wu	Wa	Wa	Wu	Wi	Wu
Wu	Wu	Wi	Wu	Wi	Wa
Wa	Wi	Wi	Wa	Wi	Wa
Wu	Wi	Wa	Wi	Wa	Wu
Wu	Wa	Wi	Wu	Wa	Wi

Read each row from right to left.

Yu	Ya	Yi	Yi	Ya	Ya
Ya	Yu	Yu	Yi	Yi	Ya
Ya	Yi	Yu	Yu	Ya	Yi
Yi	Ya	Ya	Ya	Yi	Yi
Ya	Yi	Yi	Yu	Yi	Ya
Yi	Ya	Yu	Yu	Yu	Yi
Yi	Yu	Yu	Yu	Ya	Ya

Short Vowel Exercise 2.1

Read each row from right to left.

Sa Za Du Dha Ru Sa Du DhuAa Du Ta Ii Ga Ii

Thu Ba Aa TaKhaHi Da JuZa Uu FuAa Fa Ii

Gi Ii Bu Ra Su Shu Sa Du Dhi Fu Bi

Za Uu Zu Ii Zu Aa Zi Aa Ta Ja Khu Ha Du Ru Aa Bu

Za Wi na Na Ti Ma Sha Thu Su Zi Wa Zu

Ma Ni Tu hu Su Dha Du Zu Wa Shu Ru Ba

Si Sha Sa Ki Dha Ki Du La ZuRa Ki Za

Short Vowel Exercise 2.2

Read each row from right to left.

Kha Ti Uu Ha Zu Ii Za Ii Zu Ii Za Ii Za Ii Za Ii Sa

Kha IiKhaUuKhuTa Du Ja Di Hu Tu KhaDa Ji Ha

Kha Ti DuBi Ii Tu Da KhaDi Tu Du Ja Hu DaKhu

Ti DaUu Bi Thu BaUuKhali Ju Ii Ba Thu DuDu

Ra Du RaUuRuHuKha Di Ju Hu Uu Ii Dhu Ii Dhu Dha Uu Dha

Ii AaJu Ii Ba ThaDhiJu Ha KhaUu Dhu Dhu Di Dha Tu

Ba Tha Dhu Bu Thi Ii Ru Ii RaAa Ri Ii Ra Da Ja Hu

Short Vowel Exercise 2.3

Read each row from right to left.

Sa Khi Sa Ju Si Za Su Zi Dhi Su DhiAa Su

Uu Sa Ri Su Thu Aa Su ShuAa ShaUu Shi Ii Sha

Sha Dhi Ra Sha KhuShaDha Su Di Tu Ha Uu Sa

Ii Sa IiKhuJu Ha Zu RaDhi Sa Shu Ra Su

Shu Su Thi Sa DhiAa Si Uu Ru Su Sa

Sha DhuSa Sa Du Ii Da Uu Du Ii Da

Si KhaDu Da Da Da Da Du Ru Za Ta Bu

Short Vowel Exercise 2.4

Read each row from right to left.

Tha Dhu Da Ii Su Du Ii Ta UuTa UuTu Ii Ta

Ii Sa Ta Tu Nu Ii Tu Ha Kha Ii Du Dhi Ta Da

Ja Tu Ti Za Zu Zi Ta Ii Ba ThiDhuAa ZuUuIi

Ii Za Aa Zi Ii Za Uu Ta Ju Kha Hu Di Ra Uu Ba Zu

Sha Ri Zu Ha Du Ja Ii Dhi Ra Zu Tu Ii Bu Aa

Khu Ti Hu Aa Ju IiAa Ii AaDhi Ru Ba Thu Ta

Sa Zi DaDhuRa Su Di Dhu AaDa Tu Uu Ga Ii

Short Vowel Exercise 2.5

Read each row from right to left.

Ga Aa Gi Aa Gu Dhu Si Shu Qa Su Zu Zi Qa

Sa Shu Da Tha Bu Qi Uu Tu Kha Ha Du Ja

Qa Zi Ru La Bu Qi Gu Qu Aa Tu Qi Gu Khu

Lu Wa AaUu Ya Ii Yu Uu Yu Aa YaUu Zu Wa

Qu Ga Ha Qi Ga Zi AaDhi Fi QaUu Ga Uu Fu

Tha Sa Shi Ga Aa Ba Uu Ki AaKu AaKi Ii KuAa

Ku Ra Sa Shu Sa Du Dha Ki Qu Bu Ra

Short Vowel Exercise 2.6

Read each row from right to left.

Ta Zu LaDhiAaLuAaLiUu Li Ii LuAa LaKa Bu

Sa Shu Sa Ku Dhi Ka Da La Zu Ra Ki Za

Ru Ti Ii La Ba Su Lu Thi Fa Qu Li Uu Ga

Khu Ha Da Ju Tu Za Za La Ku La Ba Lu Su Ii

Zi Ka Za Ti Ka Tu Du Ja Tu Wa Ii Bu La

Zi Wa Ii Na Tu Ma Shu Tha Sa Zu Wa Zu

Ma Na Ta ha Sa Dhu Da Zu Wi Sha Ri Ba

Short Vowel Exercise 2.7

Read each row from right to left.

Ra Ii Tha Ii Uu hu Kha Ba Mi Ki Kha Tu Za Da

Ja Du Za Ii Su Ya Dhu Ru Kha La Ii Mu Ya

Zi Zi Da Gu Wa Ya hu Aa Ti Ii Yu Bu

Sha ha Su Ba Ma Nu Tha Uu Ta Bu Ta Uu Ii

Ii Thu Ta Thi Sa Da Dhi Ra Yu Zu Wa Za

Ki Ma Da Dhu Ka Fa Bu Tu Tu Na Ii Ti Hu

Khu Ii Du Dha Ti Du Ja Ta Ra Ku Za Ti Kha

Long vowels [aa] [ee] [oo] — Practice Exercise 3.1

Read each row from right to left.

Uoo	Iee	Aaa	Iee	Aaa	Uoo
Uoo	Aaa	Iee	Uoo	Aaa	Iee
Aaa	Iee	Iee	Aaa	Iee	Aaa
Iee	Aaa	Aaa	Iee	Uoo	Aaa
Uoo	Aaa	Aaa	Uoo	Iee	Uoo
Iee	Iee	Aaa	Uoo	Aaa	Iee
Uoo	Uoo	Iee	Uoo	Iee	Aaa

Long vowels [aa] [ee] [oo] — Practice Exercise 3.2

Read each row from right to left.

Bee	Baa	Bee	Baa	Bee	Boo
Bee	Boo	Bee	Boo	Boo	Bee
Baa	Bee	Boo	Bee	Baa	Boo
Boo	Boo	Baa	Boo	Baa	Baa
Bee	Baa	Bee	Baa	Bee	Baa
Bee	Bee	Boo	Bee	Baa	Bee
Baa	Boo	Bee	Baa	Boo	Baa
Baa	Boo	Baa	Boo	Bee	Boo

Long vowels [aa] [ee] [oo] — Practice Exercise 3.3

Read each row from right to left.

Tee	Taa	Too	Tee	Too	Taa
Too	Taa	Tee	Too	Taa	Taa
Taa	Tee	Too	Tee	Taa	Taa
Too	Taa	Taa	Too	Tee	Too
Taa	Tee	Too	Taa	Tee	Tee
Tee	Tee	Tee	Taa	Too	Taa
Too	Tee	Tee	Too	Tee	Too
Too	Tee	Taa	Too	Tee	Taa

Long vowels [aa] [ee] [oo] — Practice Exercise 3.4

Read each row from right to left.

Thaa	Thee	Thoo	Thaa	Thee	Thaa
Thaa	Thee	Thaa	Thoo	Thee	Thoo
Thee	Thaa	Thoo	Thee	Thee	Thoo
Thaa	Thee	Thoo	Thaa	Thee	Thoo
Thoo	Thee	Thaa	Thoo	Thaa	Thee
Thee	Thoo	Thoo	Thee	Thee	Thaa
Thaa	Thee	Thoo	Thaa	Thoo	Thaa
Thee	Thoo	Thaa	Thoo	Thee	Thaa

Read each row from right to left.

Jaa	Jaa	Jaa	Jee	Jaa	Jee
Jee	Jaa	Joo	Jee	Jee	Joo
Joo	Jee	Jaa	Joo	Jaa	Jaa
Jaa	Joo	Jaa	Jee	Joo	Jee
Joo	Jee	Jaa	Jee	Jaa	Joo
Joo	Jee	Jee	Joo	Jee	Joo
Jaa	Joo	Jaa	Jee	Jaa	Jee

Read each row from right to left.

Haa	Hoo	Hee	Haa	Hee	Haa
Hee	Haa	Hee	Haa	Hoo	Hee
Hoo	Hee	Haa	Hoo	Hoo	Haa
Haa	Hee	Hoo	Hee	Hoo	Hee
Hee	Hoo	Hee	Hoo	Haa	Haa
Haa	Hee	Hoo	Hee	Haa	Hee
Hoo	Haa	Haa	Hee	Haa	Haa

Read each row from right to left.

Khoo	Khaa	Khoo	Khoo	Khee	Khaa
Khee	Khaa	Khoo	Khaa	Khaa	Khoo
Khoo	Khoo	Khaa	Khee	Khee	Khaa
Khaa	Khee	Khoo	Khoo	Khee	Khoo
Khee	Khee	Khoo	Khee	Khaa	Khaa
Khaa	Khoo	Khee	Khaa	Khaa	Khee
Khoo	Khaa	Khee	Khaa	Khoo	Khoo

Read each row from right to left.

Dee	Daa	Daa	Doo	Daa
Dee	Doo	Dee	Daa	Dee
Daa	Dee	Daa	Doo	Doo
Daa	Dee	Doo	Dee	Dee
Doo	Daa	Doo	Daa	Dee
Dee	Doo	Daa	Dee	Daa
Daa	Dee	Doo	Daa	Dee
Doo	Daa	Doo	Doo	Daa

Read each row from right to left.

Dhaa	Dhee	Dhaa	Dhoo	Dhaa
Dhaa	Dhee	Dhee	Dhaa	Dhee
Dhoo	Dhaa	Dhoo	Dhee	Dhoo
Dhaa	Dhee	Dhaa	Dhoo	Dhaa
Dhaa	Dhoo	Dhee	Dhoo	Dhee
Dhee	Dhee	Dhoo	Dhee	Dhoo
Dhoo	Dhoo	Dhee	Dhaa	Dhee
Dhoo	Dhaa	Dhaa	Dhoo	Dhaa

Read each row from right to left.

Raa	Roo	Raa	Ree	Ree
Ree	Raa	Ree	Raa	Roo
Raa	Ree	Roo	Ree	Raa
Roo	Raa	Raa	Ree	Roo
Ree	Ree	Roo	Raa	Ree
Raa	Ree	Ree	Roo	Raa
Ree	Ree	Raa	Ree	Roo
Roo	Raa	Roo	Roo	Raa

Read each row from right to left.

Zoo	Zaa	Zee	Zaa	Zoo	Zaa	Zee
Zee	Zoo	Zaa	Zee	Zaa	Zoo	Zoo
Zoo	Zee	Zee	Zoo	Zaa	Zee	Zaa
Zee	Zoo	Zoo	Zoo	Zaa	Zaa	Zee
Zoo	Zee	Zee	Zaa	Zoo	Zaa	Zoo
Zoo	Zaa	Zoo	Zaa	Zee	Zoo	Zee
Zaa	Zoo	Zee	Zaa	Zaa	Zee	Zaa
Zee	Zaa	Zee	Zaa	Zee	Zee	Zaa

Read each row from right to left.

Saa	See	Saa	Soo	Soo	See
See	Saa	See	Saa	Saa	Soo
See	Saa	See	Soo	See	Saa
See	Saa	Soo	See	Saa	Soo
Saa	Saa	See	Saa	Soo	See
Soo	See	Saa	See	See	Soo
Saa	Soo	See	Saa	Soo	Saa

Read each row from right to left.

Shoo	Shaa	Shoo	Shaa	Shaa
Shee	Shaa	Shaa	Shee	Shaa
Shaa	Shee	Shoo	Shaa	Shee
Shoo	Shaa	Shee	Shee	Shaa
Shee	Shoo	Shee	Shoo	Shee
Shaa	Shoo	Shaa	Shee	Shoo
Shee	Shaa	Shoo	Shee	Shee

Read each row from right to left.

Soo	Saa	Soo	See	Saa
Saa	See	Saa	Soo	See
See	Saa	See	Saa	Soo
Saa	Soo	See	Soo	See
See	Saa	Saa	Soo	Saa
Saa	See	Soo	See	Soo
See	See	Saa	Soo	See
Saa	See	See	Soo	Saa

Read each row from right to left.

Dee	Dee	Doo	Daa	Daa
Daa	Dee	Daa	Dee	Doo
Daa	Dee	Doo	Dee	Daa
Dee	Doo	Daa	Daa	Doo
Dee	Dee	Doo	Dee	Daa
Daa	Daa	Dee	Doo	Daa
Dee	Doo	Daa	Dee	Doo
Dee	Doo	Dee	Doo	Daa

Read each row from right to left.

Tee	Tee	Tee	Too	Tee	Taa
Taa	Too	Tee	Taa	Too	Tee
Taa	Taa	Taa	Too	Taa	Too
Taa	Too	Taa	Tee	Tee	Taa
Too	Taa	Too	Tee	Too	Tee
Tee	Tee	Taa	Too	Tee	Taa
Too	Taa	Too	Tee	Too	Tee

Read each row from right to left.

Zaa	Zoo	Zaa	Zee	Zoo	Zee
Zoo	Zaa	Zee	Zoo	Zee	Zoo
Zee	Zaa	Zaa	Zee	Zaa	Zaa
Zaa	Zoo	Zaa	Zaa	Zee	Zee
Zee	Zaa	Zee	Zoo	Zee	Zaa
Zoo	Zee	Zaa	Zoo	Zee	Zaa
Zaa	Zoo	Zee	Zoo	Zaa	Zee

Read each row from right to left.

Aaa	Uoo	Eee	Aaa	Aaa	Eee
Uoo	Aaa	Eee	Aaa	Eee	Uoo
Eee	Aaa	Uoo	Eee	Aaa	Uoo
Aaa	Eee	Aaa	Eee	Eee	Aaa
Eee	Aaa	Uoo	Aaa	Eee	Eee
Aaa	Eee	Uoo	Eee	Uoo	Uoo
Uoo	Eee	Uoo	Aaa	Aaa	Uoo

Read each row from right to left.

Goo	Gaa	Gee	Gaa	Gee	Gaa
Gaa	Goo	Goo	Gee	Gaa	Gee
Gee	Gaa	Gaa	Goo	Gee	Goo
Gee	Goo	Goo	Gee	Gaa	Gaa
Gee	Gee	Gee	Gaa	Goo	Goo
Gee	Gaa	Goo	Gee	Gee	Gaa
Gaa	Goo	Goo	Goo	Goo	Goo

Read each row from right to left.

Faa	Foo	Eee	Faa	Faa	Eee
Foo	Faa	Eee	Faa	Eee	Foo
Eee	Faa	Foo	Eee	Faa	Foo
Faa	Faa	Eee	Fee	Eee	Eaa
Fee	Faa	Foo	Faa	Eee	Eee
Eaa	Eee	Eee	Foo	Eee	Foo
Foo	Eee	Foo	Eaa	Faa	Foo

Practice Exercise 3.21

Read each row from right to left.

Qee	Qoo	Qaa	Qee	Qaa	Qaa
Qee	Qaa	Qoo	Qoo	Qee	Qaa
Qoo	Qaa	Qee	Qoo	Qaa	Qee
Qaa	Qee	Qaa	Qaa	Qee	Qee
Qoo	Qaa	Qee	Qee	Qee	Qaa
Qoo	Qee	Qaa	Qoo	Qoo	Qee
Qoo	Qee	Qoo	Qoo	Qaa	Qaa

Practice Exercise 3.22

Read each row from right to left.

Koo	Kaa	Kaa	Kaa	Kee	Kee
Kaa	Koo	Kaa	Kee	Koo	Kee
Kaa	Kee	Kee	Kaa	Koo	Koo
Kee	Kaa	Kee	Kee	Kaa	Kaa
Kaa	Kee	Kaa	Kee	Kee	Koo
Kee	Kaa	Kaa	Koo	Kee	Koo
Koo	Kee	Koo	Kaa	Koo	Koo

Practice Exercise 3.23

Read each row from right to left.

Lee	Laa	Laa	Lee	Loo	Laa
Loo	Lee	Laa	Lee	Laa	Loo
Loo	Laa	Lee	Loo	Laa	Lee
Laa	Lee	Lee	Laa	Lee	Laa
Lee	Lee	Laa	Loo	Laa	Lee
Loo	Loo	Lee	Loo	Lee	Laa
Loo	Laa	Laa	Loo	Lee	Loo

Practice Exercise 3.24

Read each row from right to left.

Mee	Maa	Maa	Mee	Moo	Maa
Moo	Mee	Maa	Mee	Maa	Moo
Moo	Maa	Mee	Moo	Maa	Mee
Maa	Mee	Mee	Maa	Mee	Maa
Mee	Mee	Maa	Moo	Maa	Mee
Moo	Moo	Mee	Moo	Mee	Maa
Moo	Maa	Maa	Moo	Mee	Moo

Read each row from right to left.

Noo	Naa	Nee	Naa	Nee	Naa
Naa	Noo	Nee	Naa	Noo	Nee
Naa	Nee	Noo	Nee	Noo	Naa
Nee	Naa	Naa	Nee	Naa	Nee
Naa	Nee	Noo	Naa	Nee	Nee
Nee	Naa	Noo	Nee	Noo	Noo
Nee	Noo	Noo	Naa	Noo	Naa

Read each row from right to left.

haa	haa	kee	hoo	haa
hee	hee	hoo	haa	hee
hee	hee	hoo	hoo	haa
hoo	hoo	hee	haa	hee
hoo	hee	haa	hee	hoo
hoo	hee	hee	haa	hee
hoo	haa	haa	hoo	hee

Read each row from right to left.

Wee	Wee	Waa	Woo	Waa	Wee
Wee	Waa	Waa	Wee	Woo	Waa
Woo	Waa	Waa	Woo	Wee	Woo
Woo	Woo	Wee	Woo	Wee	Waa
Waa	Wee	Wee	Waa	Wee	Waa
Woo	Wee	Waa	Wee	Waa	Woo
Woo	Waa	Wee	Woo	Waa	Wee

Read each row from right to left.

Yoo	Yaa	Yee	Yee	Yaa	Yaa
Yaa	Yoo	Yoo	Yee	Yee	Yaa
Yaa	Yee	Yoo	Yoo	Yaa	Yaa
Yee	Yaa	Yaa	Yaa	Yee	Yee
Yaa	Yee	Yee	Yoo	Yee	Yaa
Yee	Yaa	Yoo	Yoo	Yoo	Yee
Yee	Yoo	Yoo	Yee	Yaa	Yaa

Mixed Practice Exercise 3.1
Read each row from right to left.

Zaa	Ree	Dhoo	Daa	Gaa
Baa	Khaa	Doo	Waa	Yaa
Ree	Soo	Shoo	Bee	
Zaa	Dhaa	Jaa	Doo	Baa
Saa	Kee	Zee	Kaa	
Qaa	Haa	Qoo	Bee	

Mixed Practice Exercise 3.2
Read each row from right to left.

Khee	Zee	Too	Soo
Khaa	Taa	Daa	Hee
Too	Daa	Joo	Daa
Thee	Baa	Too	Dee
Ree	Khoo	Haa	Soo
Jaa	Dhaa	Dhee	Taa
Dhoo	Jaa	Roo	Haa
Saa	Ree	Dee	Khaa

Mixed Practice Exercise 3.3
Read each row from right to left.

Khaa	Soo	Zee	Dhee	Saa
Saa	Thoo	Shaa	Wee	Shaa
Khaa	Haa	Ree	Dhee	Soo
Soo	Dhaa	Saa	Soo	
Dhoo	Soo	Saa	Daa	
Dhee	Dee	Zoo	Baa	

Mixed Practice Exercise 3.4
Read each row from right to left.

Dhaa	Saa	Naa	Tee
Hoo	Taa	Khee	Dhaa
Too	Zoo	Baa	Thoo	Saa
Zaa	Zaa	Jaa	Ree	Zaa
Shaa	Roo	Too	Bee
Taa	Dhoo	Bee	Taa

Mixed Practice Exercise 3.5

Read each row from right to left.

Gee	Soo	Qaa	Qee
Shoo	Thaa	Qaa	Haa	Jaa
Lee	Boo	Qaa	Qoo
Loo	Yaa	Fee	Zoo
Haa	Zaa	Qee	Dhaa
Saa	Gaa	Shaa	Kaa

Mixed Practice Exercise 3.6

Read each row from right to left.

Hoo	haa	Nee	Mee
Ree	Baa	Joo	Hoo
Saa	Soo	Jaa	
Hee	Baa	Haa	See
Kee	Kee	Naa	Faa
Baa	Bee	Qaa	Baa

Steps in Reading Exercise 4.1

Read each row from right to left.

Zasa	Rudhi	Dhusu	Dia	Gab
Abu	Khata	DuHa	Zaa	Ii
Rugi	Sub		Shudhi	Bifu
Zua	Zui	Zaa	Jaa	DuH	Bua
Sasi	Kidh	Zilu	Karu
Qaa	Iqu	Qui	Bai

Steps in Reading Exercise 4.2

Read each row from right to left.

Khitu	Dizu	Tuza	Suzi
Khari	Datu	Dakhu	Hiju
Dutu	Dati	Juda	DaHa
Thida	Bathi	Tukha	Dida
Ridu	Khuhu	Haju	Dhusi
Jara	Dhathi	Dhiha	Tadhu
Dhuthi	Jathi	Duri	Haja
Sadha	Risa	Didha	Khahu

Steps in Reading Exercise 4.3

Read each row from right to left.

Khas	Suja	Zisu	Dhisu	Sur
Saa	Thasu	Shas	Isha	Shai
Khai	Haa	Rizu	Dhis	Sura
Sushu	Idha	Isa	Saru
Dhusha	Suj	Dhusa	Daa
Dhasi	Dad	Zur	Bata

Steps in Reading Exercise 4.4

Read each row from right to left.

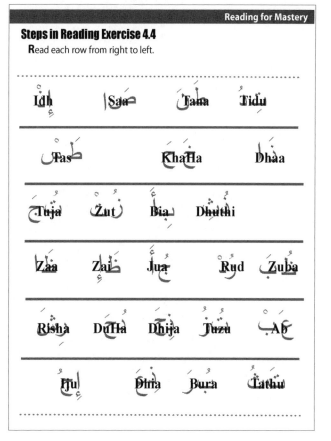

Idh	Saa	Tama	Tidu
Tas		KhaHa	Dhaa
Tuja	Zut	Bia	Dhuthi
Zaa	Zai	Jua	Rud	Zuba
Risha	DuHa	Dhija	Juzu	Ab
Iju	Dhha	Bura	Tathu

Steps in Reading Exercise 4.5

Read each row from right to left.

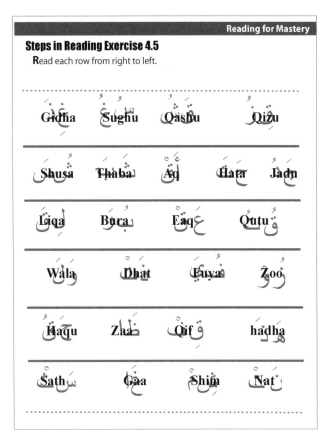

Gidha	Sughu	Qashu	Qizu
Shusa	Thaba	Aq	Hara	Jadn
Liqa	Bura	Eaq	Qutu
Wala	Dhat	Fuya	Zoo
Haqu	Zaa	Qif	hadha
Sath	Gaa	Shin	Nat

Steps in Reading Exercise 4.6

Read each row from right to left.

| Duwa | Maa | Kal | Bal |
| Hum | | Lan | La |

Did you tackle these without any trouble?
  Yes. Congratulations!
  No. If you had trouble pinpoint whether it was with letter recognition
  or the vowels and review the pratice exercises before going on.

Huwa	Lam	Dalika
Hadhihi		Doona
Tilka		Hiya
Laysa		Nahnu

Write the sound.

Qi	قِ	Sha	شَ
Ka	كَ	Zi	ظِ
Bi	بِ	Su	سُ
Ru	رُ	Za	زَ
Fi	فِ	Tu	تُ
Da	دَ	Ga	غَ
Ja	جَ	Li	لِ
Hi	حِ	Dhu	ذُ
Qu	قُ	Sa	صَ

Write the sound.

Qish	قِ شْ	Baz	بَ ظْ
Kab	كَ بْ	Sub	سُ بْ
Bil	بِ لْ	Zub	زُ بْ
Rath	رَ ثْ	Zuq	زُ قْ
Tab	تَ بْ	Tal	تَ لْ
Daf	دَ فْ	Gar	غَ رْ
Jab	جَ بْ	Laa	لَ ا
Hat	حَ تْ	Dhas	ذَ سْ
Qul	قُ لْ	Saa	صَ ا

Write the sound.

Haa	حَ ا	Bee	بِ يْ
Loo	لُ وْ	Zoo	زُ وْ
Zee	زِ يْ	Qaa	قَ ا
Thoo	ثُ وْ	Soo	صُ وْ
Tee	تِ يْ	Faa	فَ ا
Daa	دَ ا	Gee	غِ يْ
Jee	جِ يْ	Shaa	شَ ا
Qoo	قُ وْ	Koo	كُ وْ
Zaa	ظَ ا	Saa	سَ ا

Write the sound.

Shib	شِ بْ	Siza	سِ ظَ
Jabi	جَ بِ	Qub	قُ بْ
Thee	ثِ يْ	Buzu	بُ زُ
Qat	قَ تْ	Gula	غُ لَ
Loo	لُ وْ	Sabu	سَ بُ
Habi	حَ بِ	Razi	رَ زِ
Qatu	قَ تُ	Taa	تَ ا
Bak	بَ كْ	Ashar	عَشَرْ
Fusaa	فُ سَا	Saa	صَ ا

Made in the USA
Middletown, DE
14 March 2020